70 KINDS
OF PRAYERS

70

KINDS OF

PRAYERS

EDITED AND PUBLISHED BY SHEKINAH EDITIONS

WRITTEN BY PASTOR
MARIANA VANSTIPELEN

70 KINDS OF PRAYERS

Scriptures mainly quoted from King James and
New King James Versions of Th e Bible.

© 2025 By Shekinah Editions

Cover and Content Design: Marcin & Milou
Production and Printing: Shekinah Editions
Author: Mariana Vanstipelen
Publisher: Shekinah Editions
Paperback ISBN: 979-8-899-89055-0
eBook ISBN: 979-8-899-89056-7

DEDICATION

To the One who calls us to pray!

*Jesus Christ, our intercessor,
advocate, and Lord.*

*And to all who have chosen
the path of prayer,*

*May your altar always burn brightly
with the fire of prayer.*

PREFACE

Prayer is the lifeline of every believer, the divine channel through which we communicate with our Heavenly Father. It is more than just words; it is a sacred interaction that invites God into our lives, aligns us with His will, and transforms our hearts.

From the beginning of time, God has desired fellowship with His people, and prayer is one of the greatest privileges we have as His children. Through prayer, we draw near to Him, express our love, surrender our burdens, and receive divine direction.

However, many believers limit prayer to asking God for things, only turning to Him in times of crisis. While petitioning God for our needs is an essential aspect of prayer, the Scriptures reveal a much broader and richer dimension of prayer. Prayer is not a one-size-fits-all practice; it takes on different forms, expressions, and purposes depending on the situation, the burden of the heart, and the leading of the Holy Spirit.

The Bible is filled with examples of men and women who engaged in different kinds of prayer, each serving a unique role in their spiritual journey. David poured out his heart in prayers of repentance and worship, Daniel engaged in persistent intercessory prayers, Hannah travailed in prayer until her answer came, Elijah called down fire from heaven through prophetic prayer, and our Lord Jesus Himself demonstrated a life of communion with the Father through intercession, thanksgiving, and supplication.

Prayer is dynamic, powerful, and essential for walking in God's purposes.

The Apostle Paul exhorts us in **Ephesians 6:18**, *"Praying always with all prayer and supplication in the Spirit, and watching thereunto with all perseverance and supplication for all saints."*

Notice the phrase *"all prayer,"* indicating that there are diverse ways to pray. Whether it is intercession for others, warfare against the enemy, prayers of faith, or declarations of God's promises, the Bible teaches us that there are many ways to engage in prayer effectively. Understanding these different forms of prayer equips us to approach God in every situation, whether in times of joy, battle, need, or spiritual breakthrough.

This book, *70 Kinds of Prayers*, is written to help believers explore the depth of prayer and recognize that there is a prayer for every season and circumstance of life. Each chapter will introduce a specific kind of prayer, provide biblical examples, and offer practical insights on how to apply it in our daily walk with God. My prayer is that as you journey through this book, your prayer life will be strengthened, your faith will increase, and you will develop a deeper intimacy with God.

May this book ignite a passion for prayer in your heart, teach you how to stand in the gap for others, and equip you to pray with power and authority. As you learn about these 70 kinds of prayers, may the Holy Spirit guide you into a richer and more effective prayer life that brings transformation, breakthroughs, and revival.

To God be all the glory!

TABLE OF CONTENTS

PART 3: GROWING IN PRAYER

INTRODUCTION

Prayer has always been the foundation of God's work on earth. From Genesis to Revelation, we see that whenever God wants to accomplish something, He stirs His people to pray. Whether through the intercessions of Abraham, the cries of Moses, the petitions of Esther, or the prayers of the early Church, history has shown that many significant things happen in God's Kingdom through prayer.

One of the greatest revelations a believer can receive is that prayer is not just an individual act; it is a partnership with God. It is the means through which heaven's will is established on earth. Jesus taught His disciples to pray, saying, *"Thy Kingdom come, Thy will be done in earth, as it is in heaven."* (Matthew 6:10). This means that God desires His purposes to manifest in the world, and He requires willing vessels to birth them through prayer. The prayer life of a believer, therefore, is not a passive activity; it is an active participation in the divine agenda.

Throughout history, men and women who changed their generation were people of prayer. The revival in Nineveh under Jonah was triggered by a city-wide call to repentance and fasting.

Elijah, a man of fervent prayer, prayed until the heavens opened, bringing rain after three years of drought.

Daniel's consistent prayer life led to the revelation of God's plans for Israel.

Jesus Christ, our perfect example, prayed all the time; before choosing His disciples, He spent the night in prayer (Luke 6:12), and before going to the cross, He travailed in Gethsemane (Luke 22:44).

The early Church was birthed in prayer on the day of Pentecost and continued steadfastly in prayer, resulting in miracles, bold preaching, and the spread of the Gospel.

Despite these powerful examples, many believers struggle with prayer. Some find it difficult to sustain a consistent prayer life, while others feel stuck, praying the same way for years without growth. One reason for this is a limited understanding of the different dimensions of prayer.

Many only pray when they have needs, while others rely on repetitive phrases without a deeper connection to God's heart.

The Bible, however, reveals that prayer is vast; there are prayers of faith, intercession, travail, consecration, spiritual warfare, thanksgiving, prophetic prayers, and many more.

This book, *70 Kinds of Prayers*, is written to expand your horizon and understanding of prayer, and to equip you with biblical knowledge to pray effectively in every situation. Just as a skilled craftsman uses different tools for different tasks, a mature believer must know how to engage in various kinds of prayers, depending on what is needed.

There is a prayer to break strongholds, a prayer to birth revival, a prayer for divine guidance, a prayer to release God's promises, and a prayer to enforce His victory. Knowing how and when to apply each kind of prayer is what makes prayer powerful.

As you go through this book, I encourage you to allow the Holy Spirit to teach and stretch you in prayer. Prayer is not just an obligation; it is a privilege. It is an invitation to walk in deeper intimacy with God, to stand as a watchman over your family, church, and nation, and to shape the course of history through intercession.

Every sincere cry to God, every whispered petition, every bold declaration in faith has an impact, even when results are not immediately visible. The Bible assures us in **James 5:16**, *"The effectual fervent prayer of a righteous man availeth much."* This means that when prayer is done with understanding, persistence, and faith, it produces powerful results.

May this book awaken a fresh hunger for prayer in your life. May you discover new depths in prayer, unlock spiritual breakthroughs, and step into the divine authority that God has given to His children. As you learn about these 70 kinds of prayers, may your prayer life be transformed, your spirit be ignited, and your walk with God be strengthened like never before.

It is time to pray, not just as a routine, but as a lifestyle. It is time to rise as a prayer warrior, knowing that through prayer, destinies are changed, lives are saved, and nations are transformed.

Are you ready? Let's begin the journey into the depths of prayer.

PART 1

FOUNDATIONS OF PRAYER

1

THE POWER AND PURPOSE OF PRAYER

Prayer, in its simplest form, is communication with God. It is a powerful spiritual tool, one that bridges the gap between the finite human heart and the infinite, All-powerful Creator of the universe. Prayer is not just a ritualistic duty or a religious obligation; it is an opportunity to engage with the divine and experience God's presence in a transformative way. In understanding the power and purpose of prayer, we begin to realize the immense privilege it is to approach God in the way that He has invited us to do.

The Power of Prayer

Prayer is powerful because it taps into the limitless power of God.

The Bible offers numerous accounts of how prayer has changed lives, moved mountains, and altered the course of history. From the prayers of Moses that parted the Red Sea, to the cries of David in the Psalms that brought comfort and deliverance, prayer has always been a means through which God intervenes in the lives of

His people. The prayer of a righteous person is described as powerful and effective in James 5:16, which says, *"The effective, fervent prayer of a righteous man avails much."*

When we pray, we are not simply reciting words into the air. We are speaking to the Creator of the universe, who listens attentively, responds, and acts according to His will.

Prayer, therefore, is not a one-sided conversation. It is a dynamic interaction that draws us closer to God. Through prayer, we acknowledge God's sovereignty and our dependence on Him. We position ourselves in humility, recognizing that without Him, we can do nothing. At the same time, prayer aligns our will with God's, transforming us from within.

The power of prayer is not just in what we say, but in Who we are praying to. God is omnipotent, omniscient, and omnipresent. There is no limit to what He can do. Jesus emphasized this truth in Matthew 17:20 when He said, *"If you have faith as small as a mustard seed, you can say to this mountain, 'Move from here to there,' and it will move. Nothing will be impossible for you."* Prayer invites us to partner with God in bringing about His will on earth as it is in heaven. Through prayer, God moves in ways that we cannot fully understand or predict, but we trust that He works all things together for good for those who love Him (Romans 8:28).

Moreover, prayer empowers us to face challenges, obstacles, and spiritual battles. In Ephesians 6:18, Paul encourages believers to *"Praying always with all prayer and supplication in the Spirit."* Prayer equips us to stand firm against the schemes of the enemy, providing the spiritual strength needed to persevere through trials and temptations. It is through prayer that we gain courage, wisdom, and peace that surpasses understanding.

The Purpose of Prayer

While prayer is powerful, it is also purposeful. The purpose of prayer goes beyond asking God for things or requesting His intervention in our lives. It is first and foremost about building a relationship with Him.

Prayer draws us near to the heart of God, helping us to know Him more intimately. Jesus Christ modeled this relationship through His own prayers. He would often withdraw to solitary places to pray, seeking to commune with His Father (Luke 5:16).

As we spend time in prayer, we become more aligned with God's will. We learn to hear His voice and discern His guidance. Prayer transforms our hearts, bringing us into greater submission to God's purposes. As we talk with Him, we grow in trust and faith. Our desires become more in tune with His, and our hearts are shaped to reflect His love and character.

Prayer also serves as a vehicle for God's will to be accomplished on earth. In the Lord's Prayer, Jesus taught His disciples to pray, *"Your Kingdom come, Your will be done, on earth as it is in heaven"* (Matthew 6:10). Through prayer, we participate in the divine plan. God uses prayer to shape the course of human history. He uses prayer to bring about healing, deliverance, and restoration. Through prayer, we align ourselves with God's divine mission and become His instruments in the world.

Additionally, prayer is a means of intercession for others. When we pray for others, we stand in the gap, asking God to move in their lives, to heal, protect, and guide them. Intercessory prayer is a powerful form of prayer that demonstrates God's heart of love and compassion. The apostle Paul often requested the prayers of the believers for his ministry (Ephesians 6:19-20). Jesus Christ our Lord, interceded for His disciples and for the world (John 17: 9-20). Through intercession, we partner with God in His work of redemption and restoration, carrying the burdens of others before His throne of grace.

Prayer is also a form of spiritual warfare. In Ephesians 6, Paul encourages believers to put on the full armor of God and to pray in the Spirit. Prayer in this context is a weapon that we use to stand firm against the attacks of the enemy. It is through prayer that we resist the devil and draw near to God, who promises to draw near to us (James 4:7-8). Prayer helps us to maintain our spiritual integrity and stand firm in our faith.

Moreover, prayer serves as a means of thanksgiving and worship. Through prayer, we express our gratitude to God for His goodness, mercy, and faithfulness. We acknowledge His greatness and honor Him for who He is. In Philippians 4:6, Paul writes, *"Be anxious for nothing, but in everything by prayer and supplication, with thanksgiving, let your requests be made known to God,"* Prayer becomes a vehicle of praise and adoration, lifting our hearts in Worship to the One who is worthy of all honor and glory.

The power and purpose of prayer are inseparable. Through prayer, we tap into the vast power of God, drawing from His strength, wisdom, and love. We experience His transforming presence in our lives and become instruments of His will on earth. Prayer is not just a religious practice; it is a vital part of our relationship with God. It is the means by which we grow in intimacy with Him, align ourselves with His purposes, and intercede for others. Prayer changes us, it changes situations, and it opens the door for God to move in ways that are beyond our understanding. Let us therefore commit to making prayer a priority, understanding its power and purpose in our lives.

2

WHY THERE ARE DIFFERENT KINDS OF PRAYERS

Prayer is one of the most powerful spiritual disciplines given to believers. It is the means by which we communicate with God, seek His guidance, and express our hearts before Him. However, not all prayers are the same. There are various kinds of prayers that believers can offer. These prayers reflect the diverse ways in which we engage with God, and they are tailored to meet specific needs, circumstances, and purposes.

The different kinds of prayers stem from the multifaceted nature of God's relationship with His people and the various ways in which He engages with humanity. From thanksgiving to intercession, from supplication to confession, prayer encompasses a range of expressions that cover the full spectrum of human experience. The diversity of prayer reflects God's understanding of our needs and His desire for us to grow in every aspect of our relationship with Him.

1. God's Infinite Nature Requires Diverse Prayers

God is infinite, and His relationship with us is just as expansive. His nature is multifaceted, and He engages with us in different ways depending on our circumstances, our hearts, and His purposes. This requires that our prayers also reflect different aspects of His nature. In the Scriptures, we see a range of prayers that address the various dimensions of God's character: His holiness, His love, His mercy, and His sovereignty.

For instance, the *Lord's Prayer* (Matthew 6:9-13) is a comprehensive prayer that includes adoration, petition, confession, and thanksgiving. It serves as a model for all kinds of prayers, demonstrating that prayer is not limited to just one form or one purpose. Similarly, in Psalm 23, David expresses adoration and trust in God as a shepherd, highlighting the personal and intimate nature of prayer.

The diversity of prayer types allows believers to engage with God on a deeper level, acknowledging the different ways He works in our lives. Just as God is not one-dimensional, the prayers we offer to Him should not be confined to one category but should reflect the fullness of our relationship with Him.

2. Different Kinds of Prayers for Different Needs

Another reason why there are different kinds of prayers is that we, as human beings, have a wide array of needs that require distinct approaches to God. In our daily lives, we face challenges that range from personal struggles to global concerns. Each of these situations calls for a different kind of prayer. Whether we are praying for guidance, healing, protection, or forgiveness, the type of prayer we offer depends on what we need from God at that moment.

For example, when we are in need of physical or emotional healing, we might offer a prayer of *supplication*, asking God to intervene in our lives and restore us. The apostles encourage believers to pray for one another's healing (James 5:14-16). On the other hand, when we are seeking clarity or guidance in decision-making, a prayer of *petition* is appropriate, where we specifically ask God for wisdom and direction (James 1:5). Conversely, when we experience gratitude and joy, we may offer *thanksgiving prayers* (Psalm 100), acknowledging God's goodness in our lives.

Each of these different types of prayers serves to meet the varying needs we face in life. By offering a variety of prayers, we acknowledge that God is not only the answer to our spiritual needs but also to every aspect of our existence: emotionally, physically, mentally, and relationally.

3. God's Desire for a Deep and Multifaceted Relationship with Us

Prayer is not simply a transactional tool to get what we want from God. At its core, prayer is about deepening our relationship with Him. Just as human relationships have different dynamics: friendship, family, mentorship; our relationship with God is complex and multifaceted. God wants us to know Him not just as a Provider but also as a Friend, a Father, a Counselor, a Judge, and a King. The different kinds of prayers reflect these aspects of God.

When we offer prayers of *adoration*, we are recognizing God's greatness, and when we pray in *confession*, we are acknowledging His holiness and our need for His forgiveness. Through *intercessory prayer*, we participate in God's work of loving and serving others, while *thanksgiving* recognizes His daily provision and grace. Each type of prayer helps us connect with God in a way that nurtures different facets of our relationship with Him.

As with any meaningful relationship, communication with God should not be one-sided. Just as we do not limit our conversations with a loved one to just asking for things, our prayers should not be limited to mere petitions. Prayer is an opportunity to express love, gratitude, surrender, and trust, and each type of prayer helps to cultivate these virtues in our hearts.

4. Prayers Reflect Our Spiritual Growth

The different kinds of prayers also mirror our growth as believers. As we mature in our faith, we begin to understand that prayer is not just about asking God for things but about developing a deeper intimacy with Him.

In the beginning stages of our spiritual walk, we may focus primarily on prayers of *supplication*, asking God for personal needs. But as we grow in the Lord, our prayers expand to include intercession for others, worship, and thanksgiving, as we begin to recognize the broader work of God in the world.

Spiritual maturity leads us to pray not only for ourselves but also for the advancement of God's Kingdom, as seen in the prayers of the apostles (Ephesians 6:18-20). We begin to understand that prayer is not only about fulfilling our desires but aligning ourselves with God's greater purpose. Thus, the different kinds of prayers represent different stages in our spiritual development. We learn to pray more in alignment with God's will, trusting that He knows best how to answer our prayers.

5. The Diversity of Prayers Mirrors the Body of Christ

Finally, the variety of prayers mirrors the diversity within the body of Christ. Just as every believer has unique gifts and roles, our prayers also reflect our unique positions in God's Kingdom. Some are called to pray as intercessors, lifting up the needs of others. Some are called to pray with the heart of a warrior, engaging in spiritual warfare. Others may be called to pray with a heart of worship and praise, exalting God's name in adoration. Each type of prayer contributes to the building up of the body of Christ, just as each member plays a vital role in the Church.

The diversity of prayers is a beautiful expression of how God has designed the body of Christ to function in unity while maintaining diversity. Every believer can contribute to the work of prayer, whether through *petition*, *intercession*, *thanksgiving*, or *praise*. This diversity allows the body of Christ to grow stronger, more united, and more effective in its mission.

The reason there are different kinds of prayers is because prayer is a dynamic and multifaceted expression of our relationship with God. As we grow in our faith, as our needs change, and as we seek to understand God's nature more deeply, our prayers evolve. Prayer is not a rigid practice but a living conversation with

God who desires to hear from us in every way possible. The different kinds of prayers allow us to approach God in all the varied circumstances of life, making our prayer life rich, vibrant, and transformative.

3

HOW TO DISCERN THE RIGHT PRAYER FOR EACH SITUATION

In the journey of a Christian, prayer becomes an essential lifeline; an intimate dialogue with God. However, with the many types of prayer available, one of the most crucial aspects of a thriving prayer life is knowing which prayer to pray for each situation.

Sometimes, the heart may feel overwhelmed, unsure of the proper words to use, while other times, a deep sense of conviction leads us to pray for specific circumstances. Discerning the right prayer is key to seeing God's will unfold in our lives, and the Bible provides guidance on how we can achieve this.

1. Understand the Nature of Prayer and Its Different Types

The first step in discerning the right prayer for any situation is to recognize the diverse nature of prayer. The Bible teaches that there are various kinds of prayers, each designed to meet different needs or situations. Some of the most common types include:

- *Thanksgiving:* Prayers that express gratitude and worship toward God for His goodness. (Psalm 100:4)
- *Praise:* A prayer of adoration that recognizes God's majesty, power, and glory. (Psalm 145:3)
- *Confession:* A prayer acknowledging our sins and seeking God's forgiveness. (1 John 1:9)
- *Supplication:* A prayer of request or asking, often made when we need help or provision. (Philippians 4:6)
- *Intercession:* Prayers made on behalf of others, seeking God's intervention for their needs. (1 Timothy 2:1)
- *Warfare Prayer:* A prayer that fights against the forces of evil and seeks spiritual victory. (Ephesians 6:12)

Understanding these categories will help you identify what your heart needs and what the situation demands. For example, when facing personal challenges, a prayer of supplication might be appropriate. However, if you are interceding for someone else, an intercessory prayer may be required.

2. Listen to the Holy Spirit

The Holy Spirit is our ultimate guide in discerning the right prayer for each situation. Jesus Christ promised that the Holy Spirit would teach and remind us of everything He said (John 14:26). When unsure of what to pray, we can rely on the Spirit's guidance. Romans 8:26 says, "In the same way, the Spirit helps us in our weakness. We do not know what we ought to pray for, but the Spirit Himself intercedes for us through wordless groans."

When you are in the presence of the Holy Spirit, take a moment to quiet your heart and listen. Often, the Holy Spirit will prompt you with a specific prayer focus or a scripture to pray. He may also guide you to pray in tongues, which is another powerful way to pray. The key is being receptive to His voice and allowing Him to lead your prayer.

3. Discern the Needs of the Situation

Another crucial step in discerning the right prayer is assessing the situation. What is the nature of the issue? Is it for healing, spiritual warfare, relational conflict, or a financial challenge? Different situations require different types of prayers.

For Healing: If you are praying for someone's physical or emotional healing, pray a prayer of healing. Speak the Word of God over the person, such as, *"By His stripes, you are healed"* (Isaiah 53:5, 1 Peter 2:24). Pray for the restoration of health, wholeness, and strength, and ask the Holy Spirit to move powerfully in the body.

For Guidance: When making a decision or seeking direction, pray for wisdom and understanding. *"If any of you lacks wisdom, let him ask of God, who gives to all liberally"* (James 1:5). Ask God to reveal His will and guide you in every step.

For Protection: In situations where danger or spiritual attack is present, you can pray a prayer of protection, using scriptures like Psalm 91:1-2, "He who dwells in the secret place of the Most High shall abide under the shadow of the Almighty." Declare God's safeguarding power over you or others.

For Salvation: When praying for someone's salvation, pray with faith, knowing that God's will is for all to be saved. Pray that God will open their hearts to His love and truth, and that His Spirit will convict them of their need for Jesus.

4. Examine Your Heart and Align with God's Will

To pray effectively, we must also be in a right relationship with God. Jesus teaches us in Matthew 6:9-10, "This, then, is how you should pray: 'Our Father in heaven, hallowed be Your name, Your Kingdom come, Your will be done, on earth as it is in heaven.'" When discerning the right prayer, make sure your desires are aligned with God's will. This ensures that your prayers are not selfish or driven by personal gain, but rather focused on His purposes.

Spend time in prayer. Before making any request, ask God to examine your heart and make sure your prayer is in alignment with His will. When we seek to do God's will, our prayers will be answered (1 John 5:14-15).

5. Use Scripture to Guide Your Prayers

God's Word is an indispensable tool in discerning the right prayer. When praying, it is vital to pray the Scriptures because God's Word is powerful, effective, and in alignment with His will. As you read the Bible, you will find promises that can serve as the foundation for your prayers.

For instance, if you are struggling with fear, you can pray Psalm 34:4, "I sought the Lord, and He answered me; He delivered me from all my fears." Similarly, if you are asking for provision, you might pray Philippians 4:19, "And my God will meet all your needs according to the riches of His glory in Christ Jesus."

By speaking God's Word in prayer, you are declaring His promises. The Word strengthens your faith and ensures that your prayer is according to His will. This makes your prayers more powerful and effective.

6. Watch for Confirmation

Finally, after discerning the right prayer, watch for confirmation in your spirit. God will often confirm your prayer through peace in your heart, through people, or even through circumstances. Sometimes, God will bring scriptures to mind that align with the prayer you've just prayed. Other times, you may experience a deep sense of peace, knowing that the prayer has been answered before you even see the manifestation.

If you're still uncertain, do not hesitate to seek counsel from a trusted spiritual leader or prayer partner. Sometimes, they can offer insights or confirmations that can help clarify your understanding of God's will for that situation.

Discerning the right prayer for each situation requires sensitivity to the Holy Spirit, knowledge of God's Word, and a heart that is aligned with God's will. By recognizing the nature of the situation, listening to the Holy Spirit, and seeking divine wisdom, we can pray effectively and confidently. God hears our prayers and answers them in ways that are perfect, timely, and in accordance with His will. As we continue to grow in our understanding of prayer, may we become more attuned to the Holy Spirit's leading, always seeking to pray prayers that glorify God and bring His Kingdom to earth.

4

THE ROLE OF THE HOLY SPIRIT IN EFFECTIVE PRAYER

The Holy Spirit is integral to the life of a believer, especially when it comes to prayer. While prayer is the believer's direct communication with God, it is the Holy Spirit who enables, empowers, and guides that communication. When the Holy Spirit intercedes, prayer becomes a powerful, dynamic force that not only aligns us with God's will but also empowers us to pray in ways that honor God. The Holy Spirit does not only assist in prayer; He makes prayer possible. This is a vital aspect of the Christian life that should not be underestimated.

1. The Holy Spirit as Our Helper in Prayer

In John 14:16, Jesus promises that He will send the Helper, the Holy Spirit, to be with us forever. The Greek word used here, *Paraclete*. The Holy Spirit comes alongside, offering help, comfort, and encouragement. Prayer is a dialogue that requires the guidance of the Holy Spirit. The Spirit knows our needs even when we don't (Romans 8:26). He helps us articulate our deepest desires and concerns, ensuring that our prayers align with God's will.

In our own human weakness, we may not always know the right words to express in prayer. Sometimes, we are overcome with emotions, doubts, or confusion, leaving us unsure of how to pray. In these moments, the Holy Spirit steps in and intercedes for us with groanings too deep for words (Romans 8:26-27). It is through the Holy Spirit's involvement that we can pray with confidence, knowing that He takes our fragmented thoughts and converts them into a form that pleases God. This highlights the indispensable role of the Spirit in making prayer effective.

2. The Holy Spirit Prays Through Us

One of the most profound aspects of the Holy Spirit's role in prayer is that He not only helps us pray but also prays through us. In Romans 8:26-27, Paul emphasizes that the Spirit intercedes for us according to the will of God. When we pray in the Spirit, we may find ourselves praying for things we never consciously considered; matters that align with God's divine plan.

In this way, the Holy Spirit intercedes on our behalf, praying for things that transcend our understanding.

This deeper level of intercession is highlighted in 1 Corinthians 14:14-15. When we pray in tongues, we are praying directly to God through the Holy Spirit. This form of prayer, sometimes referred to as praying in the Spirit, bypasses the limitations of our natural understanding and connects our spirits directly to God. It is a form of prayer that edifies the believer, strengthening their faith and aligning their heart more closely with God's purposes.

While praying in tongues is a powerful gift of the Spirit, it is not the only way the Holy Spirit helps us in prayer. The Spirit also guides our prayers when we pray in our native language, ensuring that we pray in accordance with God's will. Without the Holy Spirit's intercession, our prayers would be limited to our human perspective, but with His help, we can pray for eternal matters that impact the Kingdom of God.

3. The Holy Spirit's Guidance in Praying the Will of God

The Holy Spirit plays a crucial role in guiding us to pray according to the will of God. As human beings, we are often swayed by our emotions, desires, or circumstances, and it is easy for our prayers to reflect these temporary things. However, God's will is eternal, and the Holy Spirit helps us navigate the complexity of life to align our prayers with the eternal purpose of God.

In 1 John 5:14-15, we are encouraged that when we ask according to God's will, we can have confidence that He hears us. But how do we know what God's will is? This is where the Holy Spirit comes in. He is the One who reveals God's heart to us. He teaches us how to pray with insight and understanding, providing us with the wisdom needed to pray in alignment with God's will, rather than just for our own desires.

In many ways, the Holy Spirit helps us filter out selfish desires or motives, redirecting our prayers toward what truly matters in the Kingdom of God. The Holy Spirit guides our hearts so that we are always praying with God's will and Kingdom in mind.

4. The Holy Spirit and Boldness in Prayer

Another significant role of the Holy Spirit in prayer is His ability to impart boldness. The Bible teaches us that the Holy Spirit empowers believers to pray with boldness and confidence before the Throne of Grace (Hebrews 4:16). The Spirit emboldens us to come before God, knowing that He is a loving Father who desires to hear our prayers. This boldness is not based on our own merit but on the Spirit's work in us. Through the Spirit, we can approach God without fear or hesitation.

Moreover, the Spirit helps us to pray with persistence. In Luke 18:1-8, The Lord Jesus teaches the parable of the persistent widow, illustrating the importance of perseverance in prayer. The Holy Spirit enables us to maintain faith and keep knowing that God will answer.

5. The Holy Spirit's Role in Empowering the Believer's Prayer Life

The Spirit's empowerment extends beyond just assisting in our individual prayers. He also empowers the Church to pray with power and effectiveness. In Acts 2:42-47, we see the early church, filled with the Holy Spirit, continually devoting themselves to prayer. It was through the Holy Spirit's power that the early church experienced miracles, signs, and wonders. The same power that raised Jesus from the dead resides in us through the Holy Spirit, and this power is vital for our prayer life to be effective.

When we are filled with the Holy Spirit, we are motivated to pray with faith, confidence, and authority. The Spirit imparts spiritual gifts to us that allow us to pray in ways that are beyond our natural capacity.

He gives us the discernment to know when to pray for healing, deliverance, wisdom, or peace. With the Spirit's power, we are no longer limited by our own understanding or ability but are able to tap into the divine power that moves mountains and brings about change.

The role of the Holy Spirit in effective prayer cannot be overstated. The Spirit is our Helper, our Intercessor, our Guide, and the source of our boldness and empowerment in prayer. It is through the Spirit that we can pray with confidence, knowing that our prayers are aligned with God's will and empowered by His presence.

In every aspect of prayer, from the words we speak to the posture of our hearts, the Holy Spirit is at work, making our communication with God both effective and transformative. Through Him, we can experience a deeper, more powerful prayer life that impacts not only our lives but also the world around us.

PART 2

THE 70 KINDS
OF PRAYERS

A

PRAYERS OF FELLOWSHIP AND COMMUNION WITH GOD

1

PRAYER OF WORSHIP
(JOHN 4:24)

The Prayer of Worship is one of the most profound forms of prayer because it transcends personal needs or desires and focuses entirely on the adoration of God. Worship is the central activity of the believer's life; it is the means through which we offer our hearts, minds, and lives to the Lord. In John 4:24, Jesus Christ declares, "God is Spirit, and those who worship Him must worship in spirit and truth." This verse is significant because it reminds us that true worship goes beyond physical or external expressions. It is a matter of the heart, a deep communion with God that transcends the natural realm and touches the divine.

The Essence of Worship

The essence of worship is about a heart that is fully devoted to God. Worship in spirit and truth involves both the inner and outer dimensions of our being. Spirit refers to the innermost part of our being, the place where the Holy Spirit dwells. Truth, on the other hand, refers to a worship that aligns with the truth of God's Word. Worship, then, is not merely an emotional response but an expression of a relationship with God that is based on His Word and empowered by His Spirit.

In the Bible, worship is often described as bowing down, offering praise, and ascribing glory to God. It is a response to the greatness, majesty, and holiness of God. When we engage in the Prayer of Worship, we enter into fellowship with God, acknowledging His sovereignty, reverence, and awe. This kind of prayer is not focused on requests but rather on God Himself, praising Him for who He is.

The Significance of Worship

Worship plays a critical role in our relationship with God. When we engage in worship, we not only give honor and glory to God, but we also receive something transformative in return. Worship has the power to realign our hearts with God's will, to strengthen our faith, and to deepen our sense of fellowship with Him. It is a spiritual exchange in which God, who is worthy of all worship, fills us with His presence, peace, and joy.

In worship, we declare the greatness of God's nature: His holiness, love, justice, and mercy. We lift up His name and recognize His supremacy over all creation. The Prayer of Worship is also a declaration of our dependence on Him. As we worship, we admit that God alone is worthy of all glory, and in doing so, we acknowledge our need for His presence and guidance.

This prayer, therefore, is a humbling act, recognizing that we, the created, have access to the Creator. The beauty of this fellowship lies in the fact that, despite His infinite greatness, God desires to be in communion with us.

Worship in Spirit and Truth

As mentioned earlier, worship must be done "in spirit and truth." This means that it is a wholehearted, sincere act. True worship is a personal, intimate expression of our love for God. Worship is an invitation for God to speak to us and reveal Himself to us, and it is equally an opportunity for us to respond in gratitude, awe, and reverence.

Worship in truth speaks to the idea that our worship is rooted in the Word of God. This ensures that our worship is not based on our emotions, preferences, or traditions, but rather is aligned with God's revealed truth. To worship in truth is to worship with an understanding of who God is, what He has done, and what He is continuing to do in our lives. It is acknowledging His authority and submitting to His sovereignty.

Examples of Worship in the Bible

Throughout Scripture, we see numerous examples of worship as an integral part of the believer's life.

In the Old Testament, the Israelites were commanded to worship God in various ways, including offering sacrifices, singing praises, and celebrating festivals. These acts were meant to glorify God and to maintain a constant connection with Him. Worship in the Old Testament was often conducted through the Levitical priesthood, but it was always centered on the acknowledgment of God's greatness and the need for atonement and repentance.

One example of worship in the Old Testament is found in the story of king David. Despite his imperfections, David was known as a man after God's own heart (Acts 13:22). His life was characterized by acts of worship and praise. He wrote many of the psalms, which are filled with expressions of adoration, thanksgiving, and surrender. In 2 Samuel 6:14, David danced before the Lord with all his might as the Ark of the Covenant was brought back to Jerusalem. His passionate worship demonstrated his deep love for God, and even though others criticized him for his exuberance, David was happy in his worship.

In the New Testament, we see our Lord Jesus Himself leading by example in worship. He frequently withdrew to solitary places to pray and commune with His Father. In Matthew 14:23, we read, "After He had dismissed them, He went up on a mountainside by Himself to pray. Later that night, He was there alone." The Son of God took time to engage in prayer and worship, seeking to maintain a close relationship with the Father.

The Apostle Paul speaks about worship in the New Testament, emphasizing that it is not only a matter of public acts of praise but also of offering our lives as living sacrifices to God. In Romans 12:1, Paul urges believers: "I beseech you therefore, brethren, by the mercies of God, that you present your bodies a living sacrifice, holy, acceptable to God, *which is* your reasonable service." Worship is thus not confined to the act of singing or praying alone; it involves living a life that reflects the glory and majesty of God in everything we do.

The Benefits of the Prayer of Worship

When we engage in the Prayer of Worship, we are drawn closer to God. Worship brings intimacy with the Father. It opens the door for God's presence to fill our hearts, and it aligns our perspective with His divine plan As we acknowledge God's greatness, problems seem smaller, and our hearts become more focused on His power and provision.

Worship also brings healing. In the presence of God, our souls find rest and renewal. Worship is a balm for the weary soul and an antidote to the stresses and anxieties of life. It is in God's presence that we experience peace that transcends all understanding (Philippians 4:7).

Moreover, worship transforms us. As we spend time in God's presence, we are changed. The more we behold God's glory, the more we become like Him. Worship purifies our hearts, renews our minds, and strengthens our spirits. It is a powerful tool for spiritual growth.

The Prayer of Worship is a vital expression of our relationship with God. It is more than just an act of praise or adoration; it is a deep and intimate conversation with the Creator of the universe. When we worship in spirit and truth, we align ourselves with God's will and open ourselves to His transformative presence. Worship allows us to experience God's glory, deepen our fellowship with Him, and be renewed in our faith.

As we learn to make worship a central part of our daily lives, we grow in our understanding of God and become more like Christ. Worship is not just something we do, it is who we are as believers. It is a lifestyle of surrender, adoration, and intimacy with the Almighty God.

The Heart of Adoration

Adoration is deeply rooted in the nature of God. It is about recognizing His attributes, His holiness, majesty, power, love, faithfulness, and sovereignty. When we engage in the prayer of adoration, we align our hearts with heaven, joining the angels and saints who continually worship Him.

Acknowledging God's Holiness:

"Holy, holy, holy is the Lord of Hosts;
The whole earth is full of His glory!" (Isaiah 6:3)

Praising His Majesty:

"Yours, O Lord, is the greatness,
The power and the glory,
The victory and the majesty;
For all that is in heaven and in earth is Yours;
Yours is the Kingdom, O Lord,
And You are exalted as Head over all." (1 Chronicles 29:11)

Declaring His Faithfulness:

"The Lord is righteous in all His ways,
Gracious in all His works. (Psalm 145:17)

Exalting His Love:

"Oh, give thanks to the Lord, for He is good!
For His mercy endures forever." (Psalm 136:1)

When we adore God, we shift our focus from ourselves to Him, reminding our souls that He is supreme over all things.

Why Adoration is Important in Prayer

The prayer of adoration strengthens our relationship with God because it:

Draws Us Closer to God: Worship brings intimacy. As we adore Him, we become more aware of His presence.

Realigns Our Perspective: When we focus on God's greatness, our issues become smaller.

Deepens Our Faith: Declaring who God is builds confidence in His ability to act on our behalf.

Brings Joy and Peace: Worship shifts our hearts from anxiety to gratitude, filling us with joy.

Glorifies God: God deserves all our praise, and adoration is an expression of our love for Him.

Examples of Prayers of Adoration

Example A:
A Prayer of Adoration for God's Holiness

Father, I come before You with a heart full of reverence. You are holy, and there is none like You. The heavens declare Your glory, and all creation worships You. I bow before You in humble adoration, lifting Your name above all names. You are righteous, just, and true in all Your ways. Be exalted in my life, O Lord. In Jesus' name, Amen.

Example B:
A Prayer of Adoration for God's Majesty

Almighty God, You reign in splendor and majesty. The earth is Your footstool, and the heavens are the work of Your hands. You are King of kings and Lord of lords. My soul magnifies You and proclaims Your greatness. All power and glory belong to You alone. Let my life be a song of worship unto You. In Jesus' name Amen.

Example C:
A Prayer of Adoration for God's Love

Gracious Father, Your love is beyond measure. You loved me before I knew You, and You continue to love me with an everlasting love. Your mercy, and Your faithfulness endure forever. I adore You for Your kindness and grace. Thank You for calling me Your own. Let my life reflect Your love. In Jesus' name, Amen.

Living a Life of Adoration

Adoration is not limited to moments of prayer; it is a lifestyle. When we cultivate a heart of Adoration, we begin to see God in everything we do. Worship through prayer transforms our daily walk with God, making every moment an opportunity to glorify Him.

Let Psalm 95:6 be a daily call to bow in worship, acknowledging our Maker in every aspect of life. May we live in awe of His greatness and continually offer Him the adoration He deserves.

2

PRAYER OF THANKSGIVING
(PSALM 107:1)

"Oh, give thanks to the Lord, for He is good!
For His mercy endures forever."

Gratitude: A Powerful Language of Heaven

Thanksgiving is a powerful spiritual weapon and a key that unlocks more of God's presence and blessings in our lives. The Bible instructs us to give thanks in everything, because God remains good, faithful, and merciful in all circumstances. Psalm 107:1 reminds us that we are to *give thanks to the Lord, for He is good!* this is a declaration of God's unchanging nature. Even when life is uncertain, God's goodness and mercy endure forever.

When we cultivate a thankful heart, we align ourselves with the will of God. Thanksgiving is not based on feelings; it is a decision of the will to acknowledge God's hand at work. Even in difficult seasons, thanksgiving brings a shift in perspective and strengthens our faith. It reminds us that we serve a good God who is full of mercy and never changes.

The Example of Jesus and the Early Church

Jesus Christ gave thanks frequently. Before multiplying the loaves and fish, He gave thanks (John 6:11). At the Last Supper, He gave thanks as He broke the bread and shared the cup with His disciples (Matthew 26:27). Thanksgiving preceded miracles, revealing to us a divine pattern: thanksgiving prepares the atmosphere for the supernatural.

The early Church followed this example. The apostle Paul often opened and closed his letters with words of thanksgiving. He wrote to the Colossians, *"Continue earnestly in prayer, being vigilant in it with thanksgiving"* (Colossians 4:2). He knew that thanksgiving was not just an afterthought; it was an essential ingredient in every prayer.

Thanksgiving Releases the Peace of God

One of the greatest benefits of thanksgiving is that it ushers in peace. Philippians 4:6-7 says, *"Be anxious for nothing, but in everything by prayer and supplication, with thanksgiving, let your requests be made known to God; and the peace of God which surpasses human understanding, will guard your hearts and minds through Christ Jesus."* When we combine our prayers with thanksgiving, worry loses its power and peace takes its place. Thanksgiving shifts our focus from the problem to the problem-Solver.

Thanksgiving also guards the heart. When we are grateful, we become less susceptible to bitterness, jealousy, pride, and doubt. Instead of questioning God's timing or fairness, we are content and hopeful. We stop comparing ourselves to others and begin to rejoice in the blessings we already have.

Thanksgiving in Every Season

Psalm 50:23 says, *"Whoever offers praise glorifies Me; And to him who orders his conduct aright I will show the salvation of God."* Offering thanksgiving when you don't feel like it, glorifies God in a profound way.

Thanksgiving is not based on what we receive, but on who God is, and what He has already done. He is always worthy of praise. He is always good. His mercy endures forever; there is never a moment in time when His mercy ceases.

Practical Ways to Develop a Thankful Life

Start and end your day with gratitude. List at least three things you are thankful for each day.

Turn complaints into praise. Whenever you feel tempted to complain, stop and thank God instead.

Include thanksgiving in every prayer. Begin your prayers by thanking God for Who He is before asking for anything.

Write down testimonies. Keep a journal of answered prayers, breakthroughs, and unexpected blessings.

Encourage others by testifying. Share with others what God has done for you and thank Him publicly.

A Thanksgiving Prayer

Heavenly Father, I thank You today for Your love, Your goodness and Your mercy that never ends. I thank You for Your faithfulness in my past, Your presence in my present, and Your promises for my future.

Thank You for life, for salvation, for provision, for protection, and for Your endless love. Help me to be thankful all the time and to live each day in an attitude of gratitude. May my thanksgiving open doors, shift atmospheres, and bring You glory.

In Jesus' name, Amen.

3

PRAYER FOR RIGHT STANDING WITH GOD
(2 CORINTHIANS 5:21)

"For He made Him who knew no sin to be sin for us,
that we might become the righteousness of God in Him."

Understanding Our Right Standing with God

Right standing with God; also called righteousness, is a gift we receive through Jesus Christ. The moment we believe in Christ, we are declared righteous. That means we are accepted, loved, forgiven, and positioned in the presence of God without guilt.

2 Corinthians 5:21 makes this truth clear: *"He made Him who knew no sin to be sin for us, that we might become the righteousness of God in Him."* Jesus took our place. He carried our sins on the cross, and in exchange, we receive His righteousness. What a divine exchange!

Righteousness Is Our New Identity

Many Christians still walk in fear and insecurity, thinking they are unworthy to approach God. But righteousness is not a feeling; it's a spiritual reality. When you are in Christ, you are no longer a sinner trying to become righteous; you are the righteousness of God living in the world. That doesn't mean you are perfect in behavior, but it means you are positioned rightly before God.

This truth gives you boldness in prayer. Hebrews 4:16 says, *"Let us therefore come boldly to the Throne of Grace, that we may obtain mercy and find grace to help in time of need."* Boldness only comes when we know we are accepted.

We no longer approach God with guilt, but with confidence in the finished work of the cross. Our right standing means we are not outside looking in; we are seated with Christ in heavenly places (Ephesians 2:6), fully loved and fully welcomed.

Walking in Righteousness Daily

Though righteousness is a position we receive by grace, we are also called to live righteously. Our actions should reflect our identity. We do not live holy to *earn* God's approval, we live holy *because* we already have it. Righteousness inspires us to walk in the Spirit, to flee from sin, and to pursue a life that honors God.

Titus 2:11-12 says, *"For the grace of God that brings salvation has appeared to all men, teaching us that, denying ungodliness and worldly lusts, we should live soberly, righteously, and Godly in the present age."* Grace doesn't excuse sin; it empowers us to overcome it.

Living in right standing also means renewing your mind daily. The enemy tries to bring condemnation, but Romans 8:1 assures us, *"There is therefore now no condemnation to those who are in Christ Jesus."* You are not under judgment; you are under grace.

Results of Right Standing with God

Confidence in Prayer: When you know you are right with God, you pray with boldness and expect results.

Peace of Mind: You are no longer striving or fearing rejection; you rest in God's love.

Freedom from Guilt: Past sins no longer define you. You walk in the freedom Christ paid for.

Fruitful Living: A righteous person bears spiritual fruit: love, joy, peace, and purity flow freely.

Effective Witness: When you live in confidence and purity, your life becomes a testimony of grace.

A Prayer for Right Standing with God

Father God, Thank You for the precious gift of righteousness. I believe that Jesus became sin for me so that I could be made right with You. I receive this righteousness not because of anything I have done, but because of what Jesus has done for me.

Help me to walk daily in this new identity. Let me not be swayed by guilt, or the lies of the enemy. Fill me with Your peace and boldness as I come into Your presence. Teach me to live in a way that reflects Your holiness and grace.

Let my life be a testimony of Your mercy and transforming power. I thank You that I am accepted, forgiven, and made whole in Christ. In Jesus' name, Amen.

4

PRAYER OF MEDITATION
(JOSHUA 1:8)

Prayer of meditation is a deep, reflective, and transformative type of prayer that allows the believer to internalize God's Word, align their thoughts with His will, and experience divine revelation. It is about dwelling in God's presence, pondering His Word, and letting it shape our hearts and minds.

The Scriptural Foundation

Joshua 1:8 states:

"This Book of the Law shall not depart from your mouth, but you shall meditate in it day and night, that you may observe to do according to all that is written in it. For then you will make your way prosperous, and then you will have good success."

This verse highlights the importance of constant meditation on God's Word. Meditation in biblical terms is not an emptying of the mind, as seen in some secular practices, but rather a filling of the mind with God's truth. It involves speaking, thinking, and contemplating His Word until it becomes part of one's daily walk and decision-making.

The Process of Meditative Prayer

1. *Selecting a Scripture:* Choose a passage from the Bible, such as Joshua 1:8, Psalm 1:2, or Philippians 4:8. The passage should be one that speaks to your current situation or spiritual growth.

2. *Reading and Repeating* Slowly read the verse, emphasizing different words to uncover deeper meaning. For instance:

   "This Book of the Law shall not depart from your mouth..."

   "...but you shall meditate in it day and night..."

   "...that you may observe to do according to all that is written in it..."

   "For then you will make your way prosperous, and then you will have good success."

3. *Pondering the Word:* Reflect on what the verse means for your life. Ask questions: What is God saying to me? How can I apply this truth today? What changes must I make in my thinking or actions?

4. *Speaking the Word in Prayer:* Turn the verse into a personal prayer: *"Lord, help me to keep Your Word in my heart. Teach me to meditate on it day and night so that I may walk in obedience and experience the success You promise."*

5. *Listening for God's Voice:* Stay in silence before God, allowing Him to impress His thoughts upon your spirit. Meditation opens the heart to divine revelation, guidance, and encouragement.

The Benefits of Meditative Prayer

Spiritual Growth: Meditation strengthens faith and deepens understanding of God's ways.

Renewed Mind: Romans 12:2 speaks of being transformed by the renewal of the mind, which meditation facilitates.

Inner Peace: Philippians 4:7 describes a peace that surpasses understanding, which comes when we meditate on God's promises.

Increased Sensitivity to the Holy Spirit: By focusing on God's Word, we become more aware of His leading and voice.

Prosperity and Success: Joshua 1:8 assures that meditating on God's Word leads to a prosperous and successful life.

Applying Meditation in Daily Life

Morning Devotion: Start the day with a Scripture, meditating on it as you pray.

Throughout the Day: Reflect on the verse during breaks, repeating it quietly.

Before Sleep: End the day with meditative prayer, allowing God's Word to settle in your heart.

The prayer of meditation is a powerful spiritual discipline that transforms the believer's heart and mind. It brings clarity, wisdom, and divine insight, leading to a life that is in harmony with God's purpose. As we meditate on God's Word Day and night, we walk in His ways, experiencing His promises and success.

5

PRAYER OF COMMUNION WITH GOD
(JAMES 4:8)

"Draw near to God,
and He will draw near to you."

The Sacred Invitation to Communion

The prayer of communion with God is the highest and most intimate form of prayer. It transcends petitions and intercessions; it is a deep yearning for the presence of God, a longing to abide in Him as He abides in us. James 4:8 extends a divine invitation to draw near to God, assuring us that He, in His infinite mercy, will draw near to us. This prayer is an act of holy surrender, an immersion into His divine presence where the soul finds its truest fulfillment.

Communion with God requires a heart purified by the blood of Jesus, hands cleansed from sin, and a spirit consecrated for His glory. It is not an exercise of words but a posture of the heart; one that seeks God for Who He is rather than for what He gives. True communion begins when we desire God above all else, when our spirit thirsts for Him as the psalmist declares: *"As the deer pants for the water brooks, so pants my soul for You, O God"* (Psalm 42:1).

The Sanctity of Dwelling in His Presence

The prayer of communion is not rushed; it is a sacred dwelling in the presence of the Almighty. Moses spent forty days on Mount Sinai communing with God, and when he descended, his face shone with divine radiance (Exodus 34:29). Likewise, when we dwell in God's presence, we are transformed. Our burdens are lifted, our spirits are renewed, and we become carriers of His glory.

To enter into deep communion with God, we must cultivate an atmosphere of holiness. This means setting apart time, removing distractions, and approaching Him with reverence. Jesus Christ demonstrated this to us, often retreating to solitary places to pray (Luke 5:16). If the Son of God sought communion with the Father, how much more should we, His children, seek Him daily?

Living a Life of Communion

The prayer of communion is not confined to moments of devotion but should permeate our daily lives. *"Pray without ceasing"* 1 Thessalonians 5:17 calls us to remain in constant fellowship with God. This is possible when our hearts are attuned to Him, when we walk in obedience, and when we carry an awareness of His abiding presence.

May our hearts continually yearn for Him. May our spirits be drawn into the depths of His love, where we are transformed in His likeness. And may we echo the words of the apostle Paul: *"That I may know Him and the power of His resurrection"* Philippians 3:10.

Let us, therefore, draw near to Him, for He is ever near to those who seek Him in holiness and truth.

B

PRAYERS OF PETITION AND SUPPLICATION

6

PRAYER OF PETITION
(MATTHEW 7:7)

Prayer is a powerful tool given to believers to communicate with God, express their desires, and align themselves with His will. Among the different kinds of prayers, the **Prayer of Petition** holds a unique place. It is the act of earnestly asking God for something specific, with the expectation that He hears and answers. In Matthew 7:7, our Lord Jesus Christ teaches, *"Ask, and it shall be given you; seek, and ye shall find; knock, and it shall be opened unto you."* This scripture reveals the three progressive levels of God's intervention: asking, seeking, and knocking; each demonstrating a deeper level of engagement in our petitions before the Lord.

Understanding the Prayer of Petition

A petition is a formal request, and when we bring our petitions before God, we are presenting our needs and desires with faith, believing that He will answer according to His perfect will. The Prayer of Petition is not just a casual asking but a heartfelt, faith-filled request that aligns with God's Word and His promises.

Jesus Christ encourages us to ask because God is a loving Father who delights in blessing His children. However, a petition must be made with the right heart, humility, and a trust that God knows what is best. James 4:3 warns, *"Ye ask, and receive not, because ye ask amiss, that ye may consume it upon your lusts."* This reminds us that our petitions should align with God's purposes rather than selfish desires.

The Three Levels of Petition in Matthew 7:7

1. Asking – The First Level of Petition

Asking is the simplest form of a petition. It involves presenting our needs to God in prayer, trusting that He hears us. Jesus Christ invites us to ask, assuring us that God responds to His children. Philippians 4:6 reinforces this by stating, *"Be careful for nothing; but in everything by prayer and supplication with thanksgiving let your requests be made known unto God."* Asking should be done with faith and expectancy, believing that God is able to provide.

2. Seeking – A Deeper Level of Petition

Seeking goes beyond asking; it involves persistence, searching, and a deeper pursuit of God's will. When we seek, we do not just ask once and forget; we actively pursue God's guidance and direction. This level of petition requires diligence, patience, and faith. Jeremiah 29:13 affirms, *"And you will seek Me and find Me, when you search for Me with all your heart."* Seeking involves studying God's Word, spending time in His presence, and allowing the Holy Spirit to reveal His answers.

3. Knocking – The Highest Level of Petition

Knocking signifies perseverance and an unyielding faith. When we knock, we are pressing in with spiritual determination, refusing to give up until the answer comes. This is the kind of prayer Jesus Christ spoke about in Luke 18:1-8, where He tells the parable of the persistent widow who kept seeking justice from the judge until she received it. Knocking requires boldness, tenacity, and unwavering trust in God's promises.

Conditions for Effective Petitions

To pray a successful Prayer of Petition, consider the following:

1. *Pray in Faith:* Hebrews 11:6 states, *"But without faith it is impossible to please Him: for he that cometh to God must believe that He is, and that He is a rewarder of them that diligently seek Him."*

2. *Align with God's Will:* 1 John 5:14-15 assures us that when we pray according to God's will, He hears us.

3. *Pray with Thanksgiving:* Philippians 4:6 encourages us to accompany our petitions with gratitude, acknowledging God's goodness.

4. *Be Persistent:* Luke 11:9-10 teaches that continuous asking, seeking, and knocking yield results.

5. *Live in Obedience:* Psalm 66:18 warns that if we regard iniquity in our hearts, God will not hear our prayers.

Some examples of Petition in the Bible

Hannah's Petition (1 Samuel 1:10-20): Hannah prayed fervently for a son, and God granted her request, giving her Samuel.

Jabez's Prayer (1 Chronicles 4:10): Jabez petitioned God to bless him and enlarge his territory, and God answered his prayer.

The Prayer of Petition is an essential aspect of a believer's prayer life. It invites us to bring our requests before God with faith, persistence, and a heart aligned with His will. As we ask, seek, and knock, we develop a deeper dependence on God and witness His faithfulness in answering our prayers. Let us boldly approach God's throne, knowing that He is our loving Father who delights in giving good gifts to His children.

7

PRAYER OF SUPPLICATION
(PHILIPPIANS 4:6)

The prayer of supplication is a heartfelt, earnest plea to God, often expressed in times of deep need, distress, or dependence on His divine intervention. Again Philippians 4:6 instructs us, *"Be anxious for nothing, but in everything by prayer and supplication, with thanksgiving, let your requests be made known to God."* This verse highlights the importance of presenting our needs before the Lord with humility, faith, and gratitude.

Understanding Supplication

The word *supplication* comes from the Latin *supplicare*, meaning "to plead humbly." In biblical terms, it signifies a deep, sincere, and persistent request made to God. Unlike casual prayers, supplication carries a sense of urgency and intensity. It is the kind of prayer that arises when one is faced with circumstances beyond human control: sickness, financial struggles, spiritual dryness, or challenges in ministry.

Supplication is seen throughout Scripture. Hannah, the mother of Samuel, poured out her heart to the Lord in supplication (1 Samuel 1:10-11). King David frequently used supplication in his prayers (Psalm 28:2, Psalm 86:6). Jesus Christ, in the Garden of Gethsemane, prayed with great supplication, crying out to the Father in agony (Luke 22:44). These examples teach us that supplication is not a sign of weakness but an act of faith and dependence on God.

How to Pray the Prayer of Supplication

1. *Acknowledge Your Need for God*: The foundation of supplication is recognizing that we cannot solve our problems alone. It requires a humble posture before the Lord, as seen in the tax collector's prayer in Luke 18:13: "God, be merciful to me, a sinner!"

2. *Be Specific in Your Requests*: Philippians 4:6 encourages us to make our requests known to God. Instead of vague prayers, express specific needs, whether for healing, provision, guidance, or deliverance.

3. *Pray with Fervency and Persistence*: The Bible encourages persistent supplication. In Luke 18:1-8, Jesus shares the parable of the persistent widow, teaching that we should keep praying until we receive an answer.

4. *Combine Supplication with Thanksgiving*: A crucial part of Philippians 4:6 is the phrase "with thanksgiving." Even as we plead with God, we should maintain an attitude of gratitude, trusting that He has done it before, He will do it again.

5. *Pray in Faith and Trust God's Timing*: Supplication should be accompanied by faith, believing that God is able and willing to help (Mark 11:24). Sometimes, answers may not come immediately, but God's timing is always perfect.

The Power of Supplication in Our Lives

Prayers of supplication bring peace to the troubled heart. Philippians 4:7 promises that when we pray in supplication, *"The peace of God, which surpasses all understanding, will guard your hearts and minds through Christ Jesus."* This means that even before we see the answer, God's peace reassures us that He is in control.

Moreover, supplication strengthens our relationship with God. It moves us beyond surface-level prayers into deeper intimacy with the Father. When we bring our burdens before Him, we experience His love, care, and faithfulness firsthand.

Finally, supplication opens doors for divine intervention. James 5:16 states, *"The effective, fervent prayer of a righteous man avails much."* When we sincerely cry out to God, He responds in ways that surpass human understanding, performing miracles, changing hearts, and aligning circumstances for His glory.

The prayer of supplication is a vital aspect of a believer's spiritual life. It teaches us to depend on God completely, to approach Him with humility, and to persist in faith. As we follow the biblical pattern of supplication; acknowledging our need, praying fervently, giving thanks, and trusting in His will; we can be assured that our prayers will reach the throne of grace and bring about transformation in our lives. Let us, therefore, not be anxious but, in everything, through prayer and supplication, make our requests known to our loving and faithful God.

8

PRAYER FOR DAILY NEEDS
(MATTHEW 6:11)

"Give us this day our daily bread."

Understanding Daily Provision

In the Lord's Prayer, Jesus Christ teaches us to ask God for our daily bread. This simple yet profound request reminds us of our dependence on God for our physical, spiritual, and emotional sustenance. Daily needs extend beyond food to include shelter, health, strength, and guidance for each day. When we pray for daily provision, we acknowledge God as our ultimate Provider.

The phrase "daily bread" echoes God's provision for Israel in the wilderness, where He provided manna each morning (Exodus 16:4). They were to collect only what they needed for the day, teaching them reliance on God's faithfulness. Likewise, Jesus Christ calls us to trust in God's provision one day at a time.

Trusting God for Every Need

Our Lord Jesus emphasized in Matthew 6:25-26 that we should not worry about what we will eat or drink because our Heavenly Father knows our needs. Just as He feeds the birds of the air, He will surely provide for His children.

However, prayer for daily needs goes beyond physical sustenance. It includes:

1. *Spiritual Nourishment:* Just as the body needs food, the soul requires the Word of God We should pray for spiritual insight, revelation, and growth in faith.
2. *Strength for the Day:* God provides the grace and wisdom needed for each day.
3. *Peace and Contentment:* Anxiety often arises from fear of lack, but Philippians 4:6-7 reminds us to bring everything before God in prayer, trusting Him for peace.

How to Pray for Daily Needs

1. *Pray with Gratitude:* Before asking, acknowledge God's past faithfulness. Thank Him for previous provisions, this builds confidence in His continued care.
2. *Be Specific in Requests:* Just as Jesus Christ healed the blind man who specifically asked for sight (Mark 10:51), we should present our needs clearly before God.
3. *Trust His Timing and Methods:* God answers in different ways; sometimes through a job opportunity, unexpected help, or even supernatural provision.

4. *Share with Others:* When God provides abundantly, He expects us to be a blessing to others. Proverbs 19:17 says that lending to the poor is like lending to the Lord, and He will repay.

As we pray, "Give us this day our daily bread," let us remember that God's provision is both practical and spiritual. He knows our needs even before we ask (Matthew 6:8), yet God desires that we come to Him daily in faith and dependence. By trusting Him, we develop a heart of gratitude and confidence that He will always sustain us.

9

PRAYER FOR GOD'S WILL TO BE DONE
(MATTHEW 6:10)

"Your Kingdom come.
Your Will be done
On earth as it is in Heaven."

Understanding God's Will

God's will refers to His sovereign purpose, and intentions for all creation. It encompasses everything from the personal to the universal, from individual lives to global events. God's will is good, perfect, and pleasing (Romans 12:2), and it is always in alignment with His holiness and righteousness.

In a more personal sense, God's will refers to His plans for each individual. While there may be general principles found in His Word that apply to all believers, God also has specific purposes for each of His children. These purposes may involve our calling, vocation, relationships, and life decisions. The prayer *"Your Will be done"* is an acknowledgment that we trust in God's wisdom and love, even when we do not fully understand His plans for us. By surrendering to His will, we are choosing to walk in His divine purpose for our lives.

The Kingdom and God's Will

In Matthew 6:10, Jesus says, *"Your Kingdom come, Your Will be done on earth as it is in heaven."* This statement emphasizes the connection between God's Kingdom and His will. The Kingdom of God represents the reign and authority of God over all creation. When we pray for God's will to be done, we are asking for His Kingdom to manifest in our lives, in our world, and in our circumstances. It is a request for His righteousness, peace, and joy to be made real in the present, as it is in heaven.

God's will being done on earth means that we submit ourselves to His rule and acknowledge that His Kingdom is the ultimate authority over all things. As believers, we are called to seek God's Kingdom first (Matthew 6:33) and to be agents of His will in the world. This means living according to His Word, advancing His purposes, and trusting Him to lead us in every decision. It also means praying for God's will to be accomplished in our families, communities, nations, and the world at large. The prayer *"Your will be done"* is not only a personal surrender but a request for God to move in the world according to His purposes.

The Role of Prayer in Aligning with God's Will

When we pray for God's will to be done, we are aligning ourselves with His eternal purposes. This act of prayer is an acknowledgment that we cannot accomplish God's will on our own strength but rely on His guidance, power, and grace. Prayer is a vital means of submitting our own desires, plans, and ambitions to God. Through prayer, we open our hearts to His leading and allow His will to shape our thoughts and actions.

In practical terms, praying for God's will to be done involves seeking His guidance through His Word, listening to the Holy Spirit, and being open to His leading in our lives. It also involves yielding our own will to His, allowing His plans to take precedence over our own.

As we grow in our relationship with God, we begin to discern His will more clearly and are better able to pray in accordance with His purposes. Jesus Christ modeled this submission to God's will in His prayer at Gethsemane, saying, *"Not my will, but Yours be done"* (Luke 22:42). His prayer is the ultimate example of surrender, and it invites us to follow His example.

Praying for God's Will in Specific Areas of Life

While the general petition for God's will to be done is powerful, it is also important to pray for His will in specific areas of life. We can ask God to reveal His will in our relationships, careers, finances, health, and spiritual growth. The Bible encourages us to pray about everything and seek God's guidance in every decision (Philippians 4:6). In these moments of prayer, we align ourselves with God's perfect will and invite Him to direct our steps.

In relationships, we can pray for God's will to be done in our marriages, families, and friendships. This may involve seeking His wisdom in how to love others, forgive those who have wronged us, and make decisions that honor Him. In our careers and vocations, we can pray for God to open doors according to His will, to lead us to the right opportunities, and to guide our actions in the workplace.

When it comes to finances, we can pray for God's provision and wisdom in managing resources. We trust that God's will is for us to be good stewards of what He has entrusted to us, and we seek His guidance in how to use our resources for His Kingdom and purposes. We can pray for God's healing, comfort, and strength, trusting that His will for us is always rooted in His love and goodness.

The prayer for God's will to be done is not just a petition but a declaration of surrender and trust. By praying for God's will to be done on earth as it is in heaven, we are acknowledging His sovereignty over all creation and submitting our own lives to His perfect plan. This prayer invites us to align ourselves with God's will, to trust Him always, and to seek His guidance in every area of life. As we grow in our relationship with God, we become more attuned to His will and more confident in our prayers. May we continue to pray, "Your will be done," with hearts that are open to His leading and surrendered to His purposes.

10

PRAYER OF DEDICATION AND CONSECRATION
(ISAIAH 6)

The prayer of dedication and consecration is one of the most powerful and intimate forms of communication between a believer and God. It is a prayer that expresses total surrender and a deliberate yielding of the heart, soul, and body to the will and purposes of God. Unlike prayers that ask for provision, protection, or healing, this kind of prayer focuses on offering ourselves fully to the Lord for His service, regardless of the cost or convenience.

To consecrate something means to set it apart for a sacred purpose. When we pray the prayer of consecration, we are giving God the right to do with us whatever He pleases. It is a selfless prayer, always yielding the sweet peace of knowing we are in God's perfect will.

The Example of Isaiah

A powerful example of dedication and consecration can be found in the call of the prophet Isaiah. In Isaiah chapter 6, we read that in the year King Uzziah died, Isaiah had a vision of the Lord sitting upon a throne, high and lifted up. He saw the seraphim crying out, *"Holy, holy, holy is the Lord of hosts; the whole earth is full of His glory."* The atmosphere was so glorious and overwhelming that Isaiah cried out in humility and repentance, acknowledging his unclean lips and dwelling among a people of unclean lips.

After the seraph touched his mouth with a live coal from the altar and declared him cleansed, a heavenly voice asked, "Whom shall I send, and who will go for Us?" Isaiah didn't wait to be pushed or coerced. His immediate response was, *"Here am I; send me"* (Isaiah 6:8).

This moment wasn't just a job acceptance; it was a total surrender. Isaiah dedicated his voice, his future, and his very life to God's mission. He consecrated himself to speak God's words, to walk God's path, and to carry God's burden, no matter the opposition he would face. This is the spirit of the prayer of dedication.

A Lifestyle, Not a One-Time Act

Praying the prayer of dedication and consecration is not a one-time event but a lifestyle. As believers, we are called to present our bodies as a living sacrifice; holy and acceptable to God, which is our reasonable service (Romans 12:1). This means that each day, in both small and great matters, we should be asking, "Lord, what would You have me do?" and then saying, "Yes, Lord, I'm willing."

Consecration affects every area of life. It means choosing God's way only. It may mean forgiving when you have every right to be angry, giving when you feel like withholding, going when you'd rather stay, or waiting when everything in you wants to run ahead.

It's a laying down of personal ambition, preference, and pride in exchange for God's plan, timing, and glory. Such a prayer is rarely prayed in a rush. It often comes after moments of deep worship, repentance, or spiritual awakening.

Dedication in the Early Church

In Acts 13:2-3, we see a beautiful example of this type of prayer in the life of Paul and Barnabas. As the believers ministered to the Lord and fasted, the Holy Spirit said, *"Separate to Me Barnabas and Saul for the work to which I have called them."* The Church didn't resist or debate. Instead, after fasting and praying, they laid hands on them and sent them.

This was not a career move or a ministry promotion; it was a solemn moment of dedication and consecration. Paul and Barnabas were being set apart for a journey that would involve both miracles and persecutions. But it began with a prayer: a moment of yielding to divine instruction.

Your Altar of Consecration

Every believer must have an altar of consecration; a personal place where you meet with God and say, "Here am I." It doesn't have to be a physical altar or a public setting. Sometimes, it's at the edge of your bed, during a quiet walk, or in the stillness of a long night of prayer. In that sacred space, your heart becomes the offering.

God is not looking for ability; He is looking for availability. The prayer of consecration says, "Lord, not my will, but Yours be done." It invites God to write His will across the pages of your life, even when you can't see what the next chapter holds.

The Fruit of Consecration

The beauty of this prayer is that it draws you into deeper fellowship with God. It unlocks a realm of intimacy where your desires begin to align with His desires. It leads to a life of purpose and peace, even in the midst of trials. Consecrated believers carry God's fragrance; they live not for applause, but for obedience.

The fruit of consecration is joy; not the fleeting kind that depends on favorable circumstances, but the abiding joy of walking closely with the Lord. There is great fulfillment in knowing you are right where God wants you to be, doing what He has asked you to do.

Practical Steps to Pray the Prayer of Dedication

1. *Begin with Worship:* Set the tone with songs or words of adoration. Let your heart become tender before the Lord.
2. *Confess and Repent:* Allow the Holy Spirit to search your heart. Release any sin, fear, or hesitation.
3. *Surrender Your Will:* Speak openly with God. Tell Him you're willing to go, stay, give, forgive, or change; whatever He wants.
4. *Listen:* After you pray, wait in silence. He may speak through a Scripture, a gentle whisper, or a sense of peace.

5. *Act in Faith:* Start walking in the direction God shows you. Dedication without obedience is incomplete.

A Sample Prayer of Dedication and Consecration

"Father, I come before You today with an open heart. I lay down my plans, my fears, my ambitions, and my own understanding. I choose Your way. I surrender my body, my thoughts, my relationships, and my future into Your hands. Use me for Your glory. Send me where You want me to go. Teach me to follow Your voice. Make me a vessel of honor, set apart for Your work. Let my life reflect Your beauty and power. I trust You with my whole being. I am Yours, now and forever. In Jesus' Precious name, Amen."

The prayer of dedication and consecration is the pathway to divine usefulness. It is where Christ lives through us. If you desire to carry God's fire, to see His hand move in and through your life, then this prayer must become familiar to your lips and sincere in your heart. Say it often. Mean it deeply. And be ready to walk in the glory that follows total surrender.

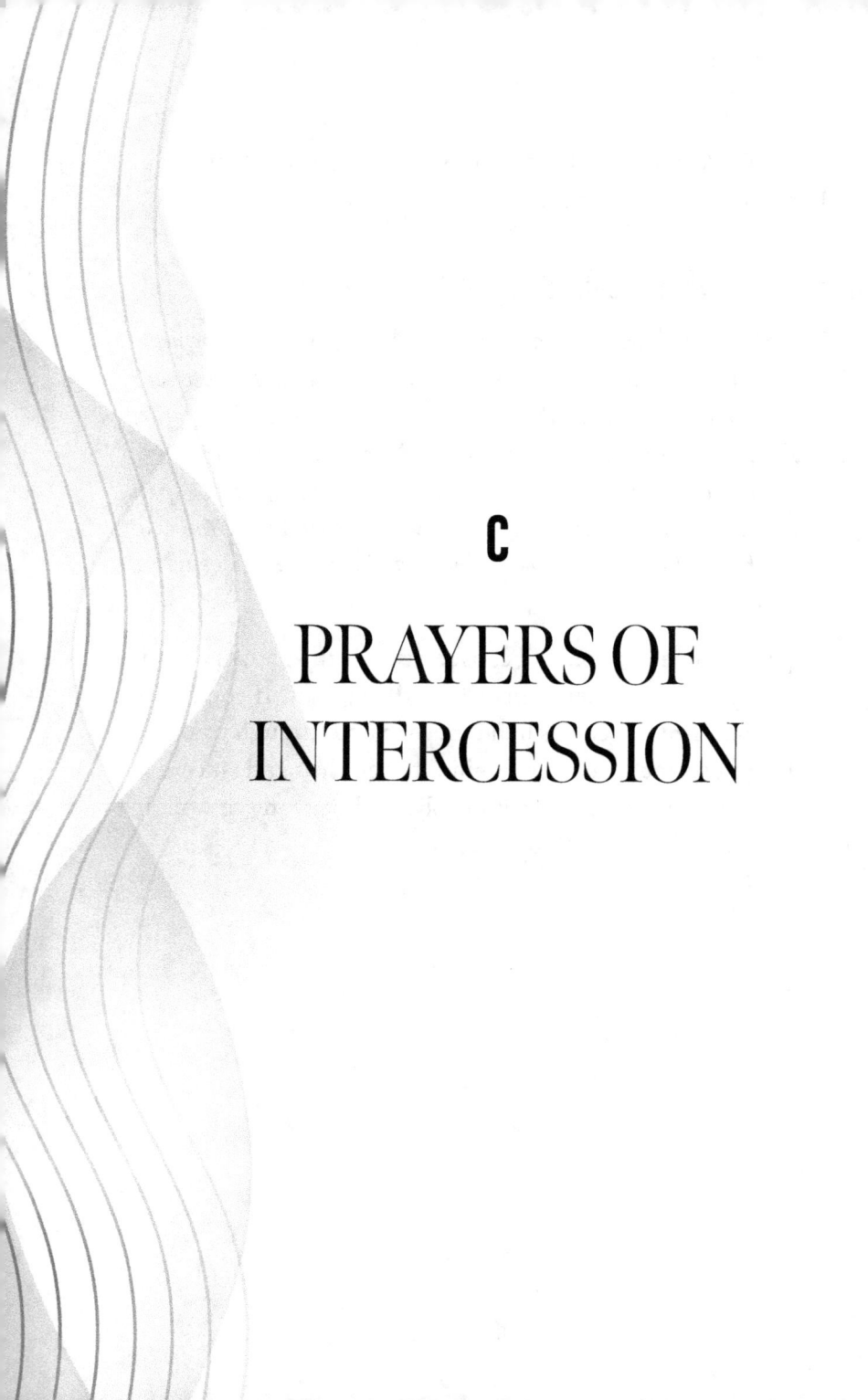

C

PRAYERS OF INTERCESSION

11

GENERAL INTERCESSORY PRAYER
(1 TIMOTHY 2:1)

Intercessory prayer, as taught in the Bible, is one of the most powerful forms of prayer, where we stand in the gap on behalf of others, bringing their needs and concerns before God. In 1 Timothy 2:1, the Apostle Paul urges believers to engage in general intercessory prayer, calling it a foundational practice in the Christian walk. This verse says:

"Therefore I exhort first of all that supplications, prayers, intercessions, and giving of thanks be made for all men" 1 Timothy 2:1

Paul begins this passage by emphasizing the importance of prayer in the life of a believer. The phrase "I exhort" expresses the urgency with which Paul calls the church to this responsibility. The use of four different terms in this verse: supplications, prayers, intercession, and thanksgiving, indicates the diversity and depth of prayer that should be involved in intercessory acts.

Understanding Intercessory Prayer

Intercessory prayer is the act of praying on behalf of others, and it involves coming into agreement with God's will for their lives. In the Old Testament, figures such as Moses, Abraham, and Daniel practiced intercession. Moses, for example, frequently stood before God to intercede for the people of Israel when they sinned. Similarly, in the New Testament, we find that Jesus Christ, the Greatest intercessor, interceded for the disciples and for us, even before His crucifixion (John 17).

Intercessory prayer is vital because it invites God's intervention in the lives of others. We pray for their healing, protection, salvation, or any specific needs they may have. Through this act, we reflect God's love for others, acknowledging that prayer is not just a personal endeavor, but one that extends to the well-being of the body of Christ and beyond.

Aspects of Prayer in 1 Timothy 2:1

1. Intercession

"Intercession" involves standing in the gap for others, pleading on their behalf. An intercessor is one who is willing to sacrifice their time and energy to pray for someone else's needs, whether they know the person personally or not. Intercessory prayer is often intense and fervent, as the intercessor seeks to see God's will done in the lives of others. As Paul urges, intercession should be made for "all people," which expands the reach of our prayers to every person, not just those we know.

2. Thanksgiving

Thanksgiving is the expression of gratitude for what God has already done and what He will do. It is a vital part of intercessory prayer because it acknowledges God's faithfulness and Goodness. When we give thanks in intercession, we are demonstrating trust in God's timing and ability to answer our prayers. Thanksgiving encourages an attitude of faith and confidence that God is at work.

The Scope of General Intercessory Prayer

One of the most striking aspects of Paul's instruction in 1 Timothy 2:1 is the breadth of its scope. He instructs believers to pray for "all people." This is an inclusive directive, highlighting that intercessory prayer is not limited to those within the church or our immediate circle but extends to everyone.

Praying for Leaders

In the verses following 1 Timothy 2:1, Paul emphasizes the importance of praying for rulers and authorities (1 Timothy 2:2). As believers, we are called to pray for governmental leaders, political figures, and anyone in authority. The goal is not just to bring requests for their welfare but to pray for their salvation and wisdom, as their leadership can impact the lives of many. By praying for leaders, we participate in God's redemptive work in the world.

Praying for All People

The instruction to pray for "all people" challenges us to broaden our prayer list to include people of different nations, ethnicities, and backgrounds. We are called to intercede for the saved and the unsaved, for the weak and the strong, for the rich and the poor. God is not willing that any should perish, and through intercessory prayer, we play a role in His plan for reaching the lost. Praying for "all people" means praying for those who may not yet know Christ, that they may come to salvation.

The Power of General Intercessory Prayer

The power of general intercessory prayer lies in its ability to move the heart of God. The Bible teaches us that God listens to the prayers of the righteous and delights in hearing us pray for others. As intercessors, we have the privilege of partnering with God in the spiritual transformation of individuals, communities, and nations. God's desire is that all people be saved and come to the knowledge of the truth (1 Timothy 2:4), and intercessory prayer is a key means through which this desire is fulfilled.

Moreover, general intercessory prayer brings spiritual breakthroughs. When we pray for others, we not only stand in the gap for them, but we also participate in God's plan for their lives. The Apostle James reminds us that *"The effective, fervent prayer of a righteous man avails much."* (James 5:16). As we pray for others, we make ourselves available to be used by God, and our prayers have the potential to impact lives in ways we may never fully understand.

General intercessory prayer is a vital practice that extends beyond our own needs and concerns, focusing on the needs of others. It involves petitioning, praying, interceding, and giving thanks for people, spanning from those closest to us to those far away, including leaders, the lost, and the suffering.

Through intercessory prayer, we engage in God's work of redemption, seeing His Kingdom come and His will be done on earth as it is in Heaven. As we pray for all people, we reflect the love and heart of God, interceding for His creation and participating in His divine plan. Let us, therefore, embrace the call to intercede for others, knowing that our prayers are both a privilege and a powerful tool in God's plan for bringing change to the world.

12

PROPHETIC INTERCESSION
(EZEKIEL 22:30)

Prophetic intercession is a deep, spiritual dimension of prayer where an intercessor stands in the gap between God and people, praying according to divine revelation. Ezekiel 22:30 states, *"So I sought for a man among them who would make a wall, and stand in the gap before Me on behalf of the land, that I should not destroy it; but I found no one."* This verse highlights God's search for individuals who will intercede on behalf of nations, communities, and individuals, to align the earth with His will and avert judgment.

The Role of the Prophetic Intercessor

A prophetic intercessor is not just someone who prays regularly but one who is divinely inspired to intercede according to the mind of God. This means praying not just general prayers, but Spirit-led prayers that declare God's purpose over situations. The intercessor perceives spiritual realities through divine insight and prays accordingly, acting as a watchman over souls, cities, and nations (Ezekiel 33:7).

Characteristics of Prophetic Intercession

Sensitivity to the Holy Spirit: The intercessor must be tuned in to the Holy Spirit's voice to discern God's burden and know how to pray effectively.

Standing in the Gap: Just as Moses interceded for Israel (Exodus 32:11-14) and Abraham for Sodom (Genesis 18:22-33), prophetic intercession involves pleading with God on behalf of others.

Authority in Prayer: Because this intercession is based on God's will, prayers are made with authority, binding and loosing according to heaven's directives (Matthew 16:19).

Spiritual Warfare: Often, prophetic intercession involves engaging in spiritual battles, breaking strongholds, and declaring God's victory over darkness (2 Corinthians 10:3-5).

Prophetic Declarations: The intercessor speaks forth God's promises and prophecies over situations, declaring His purposes with boldness (Job 22:28).

Biblical Examples of Prophetic Intercession

Elijah: He interceded for rain after a long drought, demonstrating the power of prophetic prayer (1 Kings 18:41-45).

Daniel: His intercession led to revelation and prophetic insights concerning Israel's restoration (Daniel 9:2-3, 20-23).

Jesus Christ: As the greatest intercessor, Jesus constantly prayed for His disciples and still intercedes for believers today (Luke 22:31-32, Romans 8:34).

The Need for Prophetic Intercessors Today

The world is in turmoil, and God is still seeking those who will stand in the gap. Nations are in need of divine intervention, and communities require transformation through prayer. The Church must rise with a prophetic voice in intercession to birth God's purposes, avert judgment, and release His blessings.

Prophetic intercession is not for the faint-hearted but for those who are willing to yield to God's call. It requires commitment, discernment, and boldness to pray according to divine revelation. Just as Ezekiel 22:30 expresses God's search for intercessors, He is still looking for those who will stand in the gap today. Will you answer the call?

13

TRAVAILING PRAYER
(GALATIANS 4:19)

"My little children, for whom I labor in birth again
until Christ is formed in you"

Travailing prayer is a deep, intense, and spiritual form of intercession where the believer groans, weeps, and labors in prayer, much like a woman in childbirth, until the desired breakthrough is birthed. This type of prayer is often associated with birthing spiritual transformation, revival, and divine intervention. It is a prayer of persistence, fervency, and deep commitment to seeing God's will manifest in individuals, churches, and nations.

The Biblical Foundation of Travailing Prayer

The apostle Paul uses the metaphor of childbirth to describe his deep spiritual burden for the believers in Galatia. He travailed in prayer for them until Christ was fully formed in their lives. This signifies that transformation and spiritual maturity do not happen passively but require intense spiritual labor. Travailing prayer is not a casual request before God but a deep, soul-wrenching intercession that refuses to let go until the answer comes.

The Old Testament also provides examples of this form of prayer. In Isaiah 66:8, the Bible says, *"As soon as Zion travailed, she brought forth her children."* This reveals that spiritual break-throughs, revival, and deliverance often come through travailing prayer.

Characteristics of Travailing Prayer

Deep Spiritual Burden: Travailing prayer comes from a place of deep spiritual concern, where the Holy Spirit places a burden on an individual to intercede for a person, group, or situation.

Emotional and Physical Expression: This prayer often manifests through tears, groaning, and even physical intensity, as seen in Jesus' prayer in the Garden of Gethsemane (Luke 22:44).

Perseverance in Prayer: It is not a one-time petition but a continuous pressing in until the answer is birthed.

Alignment with God's Will: Travailing prayer is about being led by the Holy Spirit to pray according to God's will (Romans 8:26-27).

Why Travailing Prayer is Necessary

For Spiritual Revival: Many revivals in history were birthed through travailing prayer, where individuals and groups labored in intercession until they saw the powerfully move of God.

For the Salvation of Souls: Just as a woman travails in labor to give birth, so must believers travail in prayer for the lost to be saved (John 3:3-5).

For Deliverance and Breakthroughs: Many strongholds and spiritual battles are only broken through intense, fervent prayer.

For the Formation of Christ in Believers: As Paul travailed for the Galatians, believers today must also labor in prayer for spiritual maturity and growth in the body of Christ.

How to Engage in Travailing Prayer

Be Sensitive to the Holy Spirit: Travailing prayer is Spirit-led, so one must be sensitive to God's prompting to engage in deep intercession.

Create a Dedicated Time for Prayer: This type of prayer requires focus and dedication, free from distractions.

Pray with Fervency and Passion: It is not passive but an intense, heart-cry prayer to God.

Use Scripture as a Foundation: Praying God's Word strengthens and aligns your travailing prayers with His promises.

Trust God for the Breakthrough: Continue pressing in faith until the answer is manifested.

Travailing prayer is a powerful, God-ordained means of bringing forth His purposes on earth. Just as a woman in labor does not stop until the child is born, so must believers persist in prayer until they see the fulfillment of God's will. May we, like Paul, labor in prayer until Christ is fully formed in us and in those for whom we intercede.

14

PRIESTLY INTERCESSION
(HEBREWS 7:25)

The concept of **priestly intercession** is a profound biblical truth that reveals the continuous work of Jesus Christ on behalf of believers. Hebrews 7:25 states:

"Therefore He is also able to save to the uttermost those who come to God through Him, since He always lives to make intercession for them."

This passage highlights Christ's eternal role as our High Priest, constantly interceding for us before the Father. Understanding this aspect of Christ's ministry strengthens our faith and gives us confidence in His ongoing work in our lives.

1. The Meaning of Priestly Intercession

Intercession is the act of standing in the gap for someone, pleading on their behalf before God. In the Old Testament, the priests interceded for Israel by offering sacrifices and prayers to atone for the sins of the people. However, their priesthood was temporary.

In contrast, Jesus, as our eternal High Priest, continues to intercede for us perpetually. His intercession is not only powerful but also effective because He offered Himself as the perfect and final sacrifice for sin (Hebrews 9:12).

Christ's priestly intercession means that He constantly presents our needs, weaknesses, and struggles before the Father. He does not just intercede for forgiveness but also for our spiritual growth, protection, and perseverance in faith. This ongoing intercession ensures that we remain connected to God and receive His grace and mercy.

2. Jesus' Intercession Brings Complete Salvation

Hebrews 7:25 assures us that Christ is able to **save to the uttermost** those who come to God through Him. The phrase *"save to the uttermost"* means that His salvation is complete, covering every aspect of our lives; spiritually, emotionally, and physically. His intercession sustains our faith and ensures that we do not fall away.

Unlike the priests of the Old Covenant, whose intercession was limited, Jesus' intercession is eternal. He intercedes for:

Our Justification: Through His atoning work, we are declared righteous before God (Romans 8:33-34).

Our Sanctification: He prays for our spiritual growth and holiness (John 17:17).

Our Protection: He intercedes for our protection from the evil one (John 17:15).

Our Endurance: Jesus Christ ensures that we remain in the faith and do not fall away (Luke 22:31-32).

3. Christ's Role as Our Advocate

Jesus is not only our Intercessor but also our Advocate (1 John 2:1). As our Advocate, He pleads our case when we sin, ensuring that we receive mercy and grace instead of condemnation. This advocacy is based on His finished work on the cross, where He paid the penalty for our sins.

The assurance of Christ's intercession should bring us great comfort. Even when we feel weak, unworthy, or discouraged, Jesus is praying for us. Just as He interceded for Peter before his denial (Luke 22:31-32), He is interceding for us today. His prayers are always heard by the Father, and they guarantee our victory in spiritual battles.

4. Responding to Christ's Intercession

Knowing that Christ is interceding for us should lead us to:

Draw Near to God: Since Christ is our Mediator, we can approach God with confidence (Hebrews 4:16).

Pray in Agreement with Him: As Jesus prays for us, we should align our prayers with His will, seeking holiness and obedience.

Trust in His Complete Salvation: Our salvation is not based on our strength but on His ongoing intercession.

Jesus' priestly intercession is one of the greatest assurances we have as believers. It reminds us that we are never alone in our prayers. He continually prays for our salvation, sanctification, and endurance. Because of His eternal priesthood, we can confidently live in faith, knowing that He is always before the Father on our behalf. Let us hold fast to our faith, knowing that our High Priest, Jesus Christ, intercedes for us without ceasing.

15

GROANING IN THE SPIRIT
(ROMANS 8:26)

One of the deepest and most profound dimensions of prayer is **groaning in the Spirit**. In Romans 8:26, the Apostle Paul writes, *"Likewise the Spirit also helps in our weaknesses. For we do not know what we should pray for as we ought, but the Spirit Himself makes intercession for us with groanings which cannot be uttered."* This verse reveals the mysterious and powerful way the Holy Spirit prays through us. It is an intense form of intercession that transcends human language, expressing deep spiritual burdens directly to God.

1. The Meaning of Groaning in the Spirit

Groaning in the Spirit is a supernatural prayer language beyond human articulation. Unlike speaking in tongues, which may involve structured expressions, groaning is an unutterable, deep yearning that comes from the innermost part of our being. This kind of prayer emerges when a believer is so burdened in the

Spirit that natural words are insufficient. It is the Spirit of God praying through us, aligning our prayers with God's perfect will.

The Greek word for "groaning" in Romans 8:26 suggests a deep, inexpressible sound; a spiritual travail that carries weight in the heavenly realm. This groaning is a spiritual phenomenon where the Spirit intercedes through us, carrying divine petitions before the Father.

2. The Holy Spirit as Our Helper in Prayer

The phrase *"the Spirit Himself makes intercession for us"* means the Holy Spirit is actively involved in our prayer life. He does not just assist us but takes over when we reach the limits of human expression. This is a divine partnership where the Spirit enables us to pray beyond our understanding, bringing forth prayers that align with God's eternal purposes.

3. Biblical Examples of Groaning in the Spirit

Throughout Scripture, we see instances of deep, groaning prayers:

Hannah (1 Samuel 1:10-13): Hannah prayed in such deep anguish that Eli, the priest, thought she was drunk. Her lips moved, but her voice was not heard—this reflects a deep, spiritual groaning before the Lord.

Jesus in Gethsemane (Luke 22:44): Jesus, in agony, prayed so intensely that His sweat became like drops of blood. This demonstrates the depth of intercession that often accompanies great spiritual travail.

Moses (Exodus 32:31-32): When Israel sinned against God, Moses pleaded passionately, willing to sacrifice himself for the sake of the people. His deep cry was a form of groaning in intercession.

4. When Does Groaning in the Spirit Happen?

Groaning in the Spirit often occurs in situations where:

- The burden for souls is overwhelming.
- A believer is interceding for a critical matter and feels the weight of divine urgency.
- The Holy Spirit wants to birth something new in the spiritual realm.
- There is intense spiritual warfare, and words are inadequate.
- A believer is in deep worship and connection with God.

5. The Effects of Groaning in the Spirit

When we yield to groaning in the Spirit, several things happen:

God's Will is Accomplished: The Holy Spirit prays in perfect agreement with the Father's will.

Deep Spiritual Breakthroughs Occur: This level of prayer often precedes major spiritual victories.

Increased Sensitivity to God: The believer becomes more attuned to the leading of the Spirit.

Intercession Beyond Human Understanding: Even when we do not fully grasp a situation, God moves powerfully through such prayers.

Groaning in the Spirit is a divine mystery, a powerful form of intercession that allows believers to pray beyond their limitations. It is not something one can force but must yield to as the Holy Spirit moves.

As we grow in our prayer life, we must be sensitive to the Spirit's leading, allowing Him to take us into deeper realms of intercession. May we be vessels through whom the Holy Spirit can groan, bringing heaven's will to earth in mighty ways.

D

PRAYERS OF SPIRITUAL WARFARE

16

PRAYER OF AUTHORITY
(LUKE 10:19)

*"Behold, I give you the authority to trample on serpents
and scorpions, and over all the power of the enemy,
and nothing shall by any means hurt you."*

Understanding the Prayer of Authority

The prayer of authority is a powerful spiritual weapon given to believers by Jesus Christ. It is a prayer rooted in the authority we have in Christ to command, declare, and enforce God's will over situations, over the enemy, and all opposing forces. Jesus gave His disciples authority over demonic powers, sickness, and all the works of darkness. This same authority is available to us today as Christians.

Luke 10:19 reveals that we have been given dominion to **trample on serpents and scorpions**; symbols of demonic powers and all the forces of darkness. This prayer is not a plea, but a declaration and enforcement of the victory already won through Jesus Christ. It is standing on the finished work of the cross and speaking with the confidence that heaven backs our words.

The Basis of Our Authority

Authority Through Christ's Victory – When Jesus died on the cross and rose again, He defeated satan and stripped him of power (Colossians 2:15). Believers share in this victory, making us more than conquerors (Romans 8:37).

Authority in the Name of Jesus – Jesus has given us the right to use His name. When we pray in His name, we invoke His authority (Philippians 2:9-11).

Authority Through the Holy Spirit – The Holy Spirit empowers us to stand boldly and exercise the authority given to us (Acts 1:8).

How to Pray with Authority

Declare God's Word Boldly – Speak the Scriptures over your life, situation, or challenge. Example: *"I declare in the name of Jesus that no weapon formed against me shall prosper"* (Isaiah 54:17).

Command the Enemy to Flee – Rebuke the devil and his works. Example: *"I command every demonic assignment against my life to be destroyed in Jesus' name."* (James 4:7).

Enforce God's Will – Speak and align every situation with God's Word. Example: *"I decree peace, healing, and restoration in my home in Jesus' name."*

Walk in Faith and Boldness – Authority is exercised in faith. Doubt weakens spiritual authority, but faith activates it (Mark 11:23).

Examples of Prayer of Authority

Breaking Spiritual Oppression:

"In the name of Jesus, I take authority over every spirit of fear, confusion, and oppression. I bind every demonic influence trying to disturb my peace and cast it out in Jesus' name."

Rebuking Sickness:

"By the stripes of Jesus, I am healed. I command every sickness and disease to leave my body now. I speak life and wholeness to every cell and organ in Jesus' name." (Isaiah 53:5)

Declaring Victory in Challenges:

"I declare that I am more than a conqueror through Christ. No obstacle shall defeat me. Every plan of the enemy is destroyed, and I walk in divine victory."

The prayer of authority is essential for every believer. It is not a weak or passive prayer but a firm declaration of our position in Christ. As we exercise our authority, we manifest the power of God in our lives and experience victory over the enemy. May we always stand boldly, knowing that through Christ, we have been given power over all the works of darkness.

17

PRAYER OF BINDING AND LOOSING
(MATTHEW 18:18)

Introduction to Binding and Loosing

The prayer of binding and loosing is a powerful spiritual weapon given to believers by Jesus Christ. In Matthew 18:18, Jesus declares, *"Assuredly, I say to you, whatever you bind on earth will be bound in heaven, and whatever you loose on earth will be loosed in heaven."* This verse emphasizes the authority given to God's children to exercise divine control over spiritual matters. The terms *binding* and *loosing* refer to prohibiting or allowing certain spiritual realities to manifest in the physical realm.

Understanding this type of prayer requires us to recognize the authority of the believer, the function of spiritual laws, and the power of agreement with heaven's will.

When we engage in the prayer of binding and loosing, we align ourselves with God's purposes, resisting the works of the enemy and releasing divine blessings.

The Authority of the Believer

Jesus granted His followers authority over the works of darkness. This is further confirmed in Luke 10:19, where He says, *"Behold, I give you authority to tread on serpents and scorpions, and over all the power of the enemy, and nothing shall by any means harm you."* This divine authority enables us to stand against principalities, powers, rulers of darkness, and spiritual wickedness in high places (Ephesians 6:12).

Binding means forbidding the enemy from operating in a specific area of life, while loosing means allowing God's divine purposes to be established.

When we use this prayer effectively, we act as enforcers of God's Kingdom, ensuring that His will is done on earth as it is in heaven (Matthew 6:10).

How to Pray the Prayer of Binding and Loosing

1. *Acknowledge God's Sovereignty:* Begin by worshiping God, declaring His greatness, and acknowledging that He has given you spiritual authority.

2. *Identify the Issue:* Clearly define the situation that requires divine intervention. This could be bondage, oppression, sickness, or a stronghold.

3. *Declare the Word of God:* Use Scripture to reinforce your prayer. For instance, if binding sickness, declare Isaiah 53:5 (*"By His stripes, we are healed"*).

4. *Bind the Work of the Enemy:* Speak with authority, commanding the forces of darkness to cease their operations. Example: *"In*

the name of Jesus, I bind every spirit of fear and oppression in my
family and cast them out of me in the Name of Jesus Christ."

5. **Loose God's Blessings:** Release God's truth, freedom, and power
   into the situation. Example: *"I loose peace, joy, and the power of the
   Holy Spirit into my life."*

6. **Seal the Prayer with Thanksgiving:** Give thanks to God for answering your prayers, trusting that His word will not return
   void (Isaiah 55:11).

Examples of Binding and Loosing in Prayer

- **Deliverance:** *"I bind the spirit of addiction over my loved one and loose
  the power of the Holy Spirit to bring freedom and transformation."*

- **Healing:** *"I bind the spirit of infirmity and disease and loose divine
  health and wholeness."*

- **Protection:** *"I bind the plans of the enemy against my life and loose
  God's angels to guard and protect me."*

The prayer of binding and loosing is a divine strategy to enforce
God's Kingdom on earth. As believers, we must use this authority
with faith and confidence, knowing that heaven backs us up when
we pray according to God's will. By exercising this prayer, we can
overcome spiritual resistance, break demonic strongholds, and
release the fullness of God's power in our lives.

18

PRAYER OF DELIVERANCE
(MARK 16:17)

Deliverance is a vital aspect of the Christian faith, as seen in the words of Jesus in Mark 16:17: *"And these signs shall follow them that believe; In my name shall they cast out devils..."* This passage affirms that deliverance is a divine right given to every believer in Christ.

Through prayer, we can invoke the power of God to set captives free, break strongholds, and release people from demonic oppression. The **prayer of deliverance** is an intentional, faith-filled supplication that calls on God's power to liberate individuals from spiritual bondage.

Understanding Deliverance Prayer

Deliverance prayer is a direct confrontation with the forces of darkness. It requires faith, spiritual authority, and persistence. The Bible teaches that satan and his demons seek to afflict, deceive, and enslave people, but through the power of Jesus' name, believers can break these chains.

Jesus Christ our Lord exercised deliverance, casting out demons and setting people free from torment. In Matthew 8:16, it is written: *"When evening had come, they brought to Him many who were demon-possessed. And He cast out the spirits with a word, and healed all who were sick."* This demonstrates that deliverance is not a human effort but a divine intervention through the authority of Christ.

Keys to Effective Deliverance Prayer

1. *Faith in the Name of Jesus* – Mark 16:17 makes it clear that deliverance happens in the name of Jesus. The authority of Jesus is the foundation for setting captives free. The name of Jesus is powerful and above all other names (Philippians 2:9-11). When we pray in His name, demons have no choice but to flee.

2. *Confession and Repentance* – Deliverance begins with acknowledging any sin, wrong covenants, or generational bondage. Confession and true repentance open the door for God's power to work unhindered (1 John 1:9).

3. *Breaking Legal Rights of the Enemy* – The enemy gains access to people's lives through sin, generational curses, fear, or unforgiveness. During deliverance prayer, it is crucial to renounce any past agreements with the kingdom of darkness and declare freedom in Christ (Colossians 2:14-15).

4. *Declaring the Word of God* – The Word of God is a weapon against demonic forces. Speaking scriptures such as Luke

10:19 (authority over serpents and scorpions) and Isaiah 54:17 (no weapon formed against you shall prosper) reinforces divine protection and power over the enemy.

5. *Filling the Empty Space* – After deliverance, it is essential to be filled with the Holy Spirit, prayer, and God's Word. Jesus warning in Matthew 12:43-45

Steps to Pray a Deliverance Prayer

Begin with Worship and Thanksgiving: Praise God for His power and invite the Holy Spirit to take control of the prayer session.

Confess Any Known Sins: Ask for forgiveness and renounce any agreements with the enemy.

Take Authority in Jesus' Name: Declare that every power of darkness has no hold over you or the person you are praying for.

Command the demonic powers to Leave: Speak directly against any stronghold, declaring the authority of Jesus to break them.

Seal the Deliverance with the Blood of Jesus: Declare protection and ask the Holy Spirit to fill the person with God's presence.

Thank God for Victory: Rejoice and affirm the freedom Christ has given.

The **prayer of deliverance** is a powerful tool in the believer's life. It is an expression of God's Kingdom authority manifesting on earth. As Mark 16:17 affirms, every believer has been given the power to cast out devils and walk in the victory of Christ.

Through faith, confession, authority, and the Word of God, deliverance prayer brings freedom to those bound by spiritual oppression, leading them into the glorious liberty of the children of God (Romans 8:21).

19

WARFARE PRAYER AGAINST THE ENEMY
(EPHESIANS 6:12)

Ephesians 6:12 declares, *"For we do not wrestle against flesh and blood, but against principalities, against powers, against the rulers of the darkness of this age, against spiritual hosts of wickedness in the heavenly places."* This scripture reveals the nature of our spiritual battle. As believers, we must engage in warfare prayer to stand against the works of darkness, enforce the victory of Christ, and walk in the authority given to us by God.

Understanding Spiritual Warfare

Spiritual warfare is a reality in the life of every Christian. The enemy, satan, constantly seeks to oppose God's people, hinder their progress, and deceive them into defeat. However, God has equipped us with spiritual armor and weapons to fight and overcome. Warfare prayer is one of the most powerful tools in our arsenal, enabling us to pull down strongholds (2 Corinthians 10:4) and resist the devil (James 4:7).

The Armor of God in Warfare Prayer

Ephesians 6:13-18 outlines the full armor of God, which is essential in warfare prayer:

1. *The Belt of Truth;* We must stand on God's truth to expose and reject the lies of the enemy.

2. *The Breastplate of Righteousness;* Our righteousness in Christ protects our hearts from guilt, condemnation, and accusations.

3. *The Shoes of the Gospel of Peace;* We Walk in authority, bringing God's peace wherever we go.

4. *The Shield of Faith;* With faith, we quench the fiery darts of the wicked one.

5. *The Helmet of Salvation;* A renewed mind in Christ guards us against deception.

6. *The Sword of the Spirit (God's Word);* The Word of God is a powerful weapon to counter satan's attacks.

7. *Praying Always in the Spirit;* Prayer is the battlefield where victory is secured.

Warfare Prayer Strategy

To effectively engage in warfare prayer, follow these strategic steps:

1. Acknowledge God's Sovereignty

Start by exalting and glorifying God. Declare His power, might, and dominion over all things.

"Lord, You are the Almighty, the King of Glory, strong and mighty in battle. No weapon formed against me shall prosper. You have given me victory through Christ Jesus."

2. Repentance and Cleansing

Confess any known sin and ask the Lord to cleanse you. The enemy uses unconfessed sin as a legal ground to attack believers.

"Father, I repent of any sin in my life. Wash me in the blood of Jesus and cleanse me from all unrighteousness. I break any foothold of the enemy in my life."

3. Take Authority Over the Enemy

Use the authority given to you in Christ (Luke 10:19) to rebuke and cast down demonic forces.

"In the name of Jesus, I bind and rebuke every demonic force assigned against me, my family, and my ministry. I declare that every scheme of the enemy is exposed and destroyed by the power of God in the Mighty Name of Jesus Christ."

4. Declare God's Word Against the Enemy

Proclaim scriptures that affirm your victory over satan.

"It is written: 'No weapon formed against me shall prosper' (Isaiah 54:17). It is written: 'The Lord will fight for me, and I shall hold my peace' (Exodus 14:14). I stand on the promises of God and decree that I am more than a conqueror in Christ."

5. Break Curses and Evil Assignments

Cancel every plan of the enemy and break generational curses in Jesus' name.

"I break every curse spoken against me, my family, and my destiny. I nullify every evil pronouncement and assignment by the blood of Jesus. I decree that I am free from every bondage and yoke of darkness."

6. Release the Fire of God Against the Enemy

Call upon the fire of the Holy Spirit to consume every demonic work.

"Father, release Your Holy fire to consume every demonic altar, every stronghold, and every work of darkness against my life. Let the fire of the Holy Spirit destroy all satanic opposition."

7. Put on the Full Armor of God

Daily, declare that you are clothed with God's armor and walk in divine protection.

"Lord, I put on the whole armor of God. I stand in truth, righteousness, peace, faith, salvation, and the power of Your Word. No evil shall befall me, nor shall any plague come near my dwelling (Psalm 91:10)."

8. Cover Yourself, Family, and Possessions with the Blood of Jesus

The blood of Jesus is a protective covering against the enemy's attacks.

"I cover myself, my family, my home, and everything that concerns me with the precious blood of Jesus. No evil shall come near me, for I am hidden with Christ in God."

9. Declare Victory and Give Thanks

End your warfare prayer by thanking God for victory and protection.

"Thank You, Lord, for answering my prayers. I walk in divine victory, authority, and dominion. No power of darkness can prevail against me,

for greater is He that is in me than he that is in the world (1 John 4:4). Amen!"

Warfare prayer is not an occasional practice but a lifestyle. We must remain vigilant, standing firm in faith, and continuously enforcing Christ's victory over the enemy. Through prayer, we push back darkness, break chains, and establish God's Kingdom in our lives and territories. As we engage in spiritual warfare, let us remember that the battle belongs to the Lord, and in Him, we are more than conquerors!

20

PRAYER FOR BREAKING STRONGHOLDS
(2 CORINTHIANS 10:4)

"For the weapons of our warfare are not carnal,
but mighty through God to the pulling down of strongholds."

Understanding Strongholds

Astronghold is a fortified place in the spiritual realm that hinders the freedom and progress of a believer. Strongholds can be personal, manifesting in negative thought patterns, sinful habits, fear, doubt, or addiction; or they can be external, affecting families, communities, and even nations. These strongholds are deeply rooted and often reinforced by lies from the enemy, keeping people bound and unable to fully walk in the liberty Christ has provided.

The Bible makes it clear that we are engaged in spiritual warfare. However, our battle is not fought with physical weapons but with divine weapons that demolish these strongholds. The Word of God, prayer, fasting, and faith in Christ are powerful tools for breaking these spiritual barriers and bringing deliverance.

Identifying Spiritual Strongholds

Before engaging in prayer to break strongholds, it is essential to identify them. Ask the Holy Spirit to reveal any stronghold in your life or those you are interceding for. Some common strongholds include:

- *Fear and Anxiety*; Living in constant worry and doubt, unable to trust God's promises.
- *Addictions*; Dependency on substances, habits, or behaviors that take the place of God.
- *Unforgiveness and Bitterness*; Holding on to past hurts, which become spiritual chains.
- *Generational Curses*; Patterns of, sickness, or bondage passed down in families.
- *False Beliefs and Doctrines;* Being led by lies that contradict God's truth.
- *Spiritual Apathy*; A lukewarm spirit that resists prayer, worship, and the Word of God.

Once these strongholds are identified, we can begin to tear them down through strategic, faith-filled prayer.

Praying to Break Strongholds

1. Repentance and Surrender

Heavenly Father, I come before You in humility, acknowledging that You are Almighty. I repent of any sin, wrong beliefs, or behaviors that have given the enemy a foothold in my life. I surrender every area of my life to You, Lord, and I ask You to cleanse me with the blood of Jesus. Expose every lie of the enemy and replace it with Your truth.

2. Declaring the Power of God's Word

Lord, Your Word declares that the weapons of our warfare are mighty through You to pull down strongholds. I stand on Your promises, declaring that every stronghold in my life must bow to the name of Jesus. I renounce fear, doubt, addiction, and every negative pattern that has taken root in my life. Let every lie be exposed and replaced with the truth of Your Word.

3. Breaking Chains and Binding the Enemy

In the mighty name of Jesus, I break every chain of oppression, addiction, and sin. I bind every demonic force that has held me or my loved ones captive. By the authority of Jesus Christ, I command every stronghold to fall. I release myself from every generational curse and decree that I am free indeed, for whom the Son sets free is free indeed (John 8:36).

4. Releasing the Holy Spirit's Power

Holy Spirit, fill every area that was once occupied by strongholds. Renew my mind with Your truth. Strengthen me to walk in righteousness and victory. Let Your presence drive out every darkness and let Your light shine in me. Empower me to stay rooted in prayer, in Your Word, and in faith so that I remain victorious.

Walking in Continuous Victory

Breaking strongholds is not a one-time event but a continuous process of renewal. Keep standing on the Word, guard your thoughts, and remain steadfast in prayer. Engage in praise and worship, as these are also weapons that break chains. Surround yourself with Godly people and fellowship with believers who will encourage you in your spiritual journey.

As you persist in faith, every stronghold will crumble, and you will walk in the freedom and victory that Jesus Christ has secured for you. Amen!

E

PRAYERS FOR GUIDANCE AND REVELATION

21

PRAYER FOR WISDOM
(JAMES 1:5)

Wisdom is one of the greatest treasures a believer can receive from God. It is more precious than gold and silver (Proverbs 3:13-15) and is essential for navigating life daily, making Godly decisions, and fulfilling God's purpose. James 1:5 encourages us with a profound promise:

"If any of you lacks wisdom, let him ask of God, Who gives to all liberally and without reproach, and it will be given to him."

This verse assures us that God is generous in granting wisdom to those who seek Him sincerely. The prayer for wisdom is not just a request for knowledge but an earnest desire to receive divine insight, discernment, and understanding.

1. The Need for Wisdom

Wisdom is the principal thing (Proverbs 4:7). Without it, people can make wrong choices, fall into deception, and struggle in their walk with God. Wisdom is crucial in different aspects of life:

- *Spiritual Growth:* Understanding God's will and walking in obedience.
- *Decision-Making:* Choosing the right path in personal and ministry life.
- *Relationships:* Handling conflicts with love, grace, and discernment.
- *Leadership:* Guiding others with Godly wisdom and avoiding pitfalls.
- *And more.*

Solomon, the wisest king, understood this need and prayed for wisdom instead of riches or power (1 Kings 3:9). His example teaches us that wisdom is foundational to fulfilling God's purpose.

2. Praying for Wisdom According to James 1:5

James instructs us to ask for wisdom with faith and confidence, believing that God will answer. Here are key principles in praying for wisdom:

1. *Recognizing The Need;* Humility is the first step in receiving wisdom. We must acknowledge our limitations and dependence on God (Proverbs 3:5-6).
2. *Asking in Faith*; James 1:6 warns against doubting. When we pray, we must believe that God hears and answers.
3. *Seeking Through the Word;* God's wisdom is revealed in His Word (Psalm 119:105). Praying with Scripture aligns us with divine wisdom.

4. *Listening to the Holy Spirit*; The Spirit of wisdom and revelation (Ephesians 1:17) guides us in truth and decision-making.

5. *Applying Wisdom in Obedience*; Wisdom is not just about knowing; it is about doing (Matthew 7:24-25). We must act on God's direction.

3. Biblical Examples of Those Who Prayed for Wisdom

- *Solomon (1 Kings 3:9-12):* God granted him wisdom, which made him a great king.

- *Daniel (Daniel 2:20-23):* In times of crisis, he sought God's wisdom, and God revealed mysteries to him.

- *Paul (Ephesians 1:17-19):* He prayed for the Church to receive wisdom and revelation in knowing Christ.

4. The Fruits of Wisdom

When we pray for and receive wisdom, it manifests in our lives through:

- *Peace and Order (James 3:17)*; God's wisdom is pure, peaceable, and full of mercy.

- *Spiritual Maturity (Colossians 1:9-10)*; A deeper understanding of God's will.

- *Effective Ministry (Acts 6:3, 10)*; Wisdom enables us to serve effectively.

- *Success in Life (Proverbs 24:3-4)*; Wise decisions lead to stability and prosperity.

5. A Prayer for Wisdom

Heavenly Father, I come before You, acknowledging my need for wisdom. Your Word promises that if I ask, You will give generously and without reproach. Lord, grant me wisdom in my decisions, my relationships, and my walk with You.

Let my heart be filled with the Spirit of wisdom and revelation so that I may know You more deeply. Guide me by Your Holy Spirit and help me to apply wisdom in every aspect of my life. I trust in Your faithfulness, and I receive Your wisdom by faith. In Jesus' precious name, Amen.

The prayer for wisdom is a vital and continuous request for every believer. As we seek God for wisdom daily, He will direct our steps, enlighten our understanding, and equip us to live in His purpose. May we always desire and cherish this precious gift from God.

22

PRAYER FOR REVELATION KNOWLEDGE
(EPHESIANS 1:17-18)

The apostle Paul's prayer in Ephesians 1:17-18 is one of the most profound intercessory prayers recorded in Scripture. He prayed:

"That the God of our Lord Jesus Christ, the Father of glory, may give to you the Spirit of wisdom and revelation in the knowledge of Him, [18] *the eyes of your understanding being enlightened; that you may know what is the hope of His calling, what are the riches of the glory of His inheritance in the saints."*

The Need for Revelation Knowledge

Revelation knowledge is different from intellectual understanding. It is the unveiling of spiritual truths by the Holy Spirit, enabling believers to perceive and grasp the deep things of God. Many Christians struggle in their walk of faith because they lack revelation knowledge. They may read the Bible, but without the Spirit of wisdom and revelation, the deeper truths remain hidden.

Paul understood this and therefore prayed that the believers in Ephesus would receive divine enlightenment. This prayer is not just for them but for all believers who desire to grow in their spiritual walk and fulfill their calling in Christ.

The Spirit of Wisdom and Revelation

The Spirit of wisdom and revelation is the Holy Spirit Himself, who unveils the mysteries of the Kingdom to those who seek God wholeheartedly. Wisdom allows believers to apply divine principles accurately, while revelation brings clarity to God's purposes and will.

Jesus told His disciples, *"It is given unto you to know the mysteries of the Kingdom of heaven, but to them it is not given"* (Matthew 13:11). This means that divine revelation is granted to those who are in Christ and walk in obedience to Him.

The Eyes of Your Understanding Being Enlightened

Spiritual blindness is a major hindrance to growth. With divine illumination, believers receive God's best for their lives. When the eyes of understanding are opened, the believer gains insight into:

- *The Hope of His Calling;* Understanding God's plan and purpose for their life.
- *The Riches of His Inheritance;* Knowing the glorious blessings that belong to the saints.
- *The Exceeding Greatness of His Power;* Experiencing the resurrection power of Christ at work in them.

Praying for Revelation Knowledge

To walk in revelation knowledge, one must cultivate a life of prayer. Here is a prayer based on Ephesians 1:17-18:

Heavenly Father, I ask that You grant me the Spirit of wisdom and revelation in the knowledge of You. Open the eyes of my understanding that I may see the hope of Your calling. Help me to comprehend the riches of the glorious inheritance You have for me as a saint. Let me walk in the fullness of Your power, experiencing divine guidance, supernatural insight, and deep intimacy with You. In Jesus' Name, Amen.

Walking in the Light of Revelation

Receiving revelation knowledge is not a one-time experience but a continuous journey. Believers must:

Abide in the Word; Regularly meditate on Scripture.

Be Led by the Holy Spirit; Yield to His guidance.

Stay in Prayer; Seek God earnestly for deeper understanding.

Live in Obedience; Apply revealed truths in daily life.

As we pray and seek God for revelation knowledge, we will grow in spiritual maturity and walk in the fullness of our divine calling.

23

PRAYER FOR DISCERNMENT
(PHILIPPIANS 1:9-10)

Discernment is a vital aspect of a believer's walk with God. The apostle Paul, in Philippians 1:9-10, prays for the church in Philippi, saying:

"And this I pray, that your love may abound still more and more in knowledge and all discernment, ¹⁰ that you may approve the things that are excellent, that you may be sincere and without offense till the day of Christ."

This passage reveals that discernment is closely tied to love and knowledge. As Christians, we need discernment to make choices that align with God's will, to distinguish between truth and deception, and to grow in spiritual maturity.

The Need for Discernment in a Believer's Life

To Differentiate Between Good and Evil.

Hebrews 5:14 states, *"But strong meat belongeth to them that are of full age, even those who by reason of use have their senses exercised to discern both good and evil.*" (KJV) Spiritual maturity enables us to recognize and choose what is right and reject what is wrong.

To Make Godly Decisions.

Life presents us with numerous choices. Proverbs 3:5-6 instructs us to trust in the Lord and lean not on our own understanding but to acknowledge Him in all our ways so He can direct our paths. Prayer for discernment helps us submit to God's wisdom rather than our human reasoning.

To Test spirits and teachings.

The Bible warns against false prophets and deceitful spirits. 1 John 4:1 says, *"Beloved, believe not every spirit, but try the spirits whether they are of God: because many false prophets are gone out into the world."* A discerning spirit enables believers to distinguish between teachings that are truly from God and those that are not.

How to Pray for Discernment

1. Pray for an Increase in Love and Knowledge

Paul's prayer in Philippians 1:9 highlights that discernment flows from a deep love and understanding of God's truth. Pray that your love for God and others may abound more and more in true knowledge and insight.

2. Ask for the Guidance of the Holy Spirit

The Holy Spirit is the Spirit of truth Who leads us into all truth (John 16:13). Ask God to open your spiritual eyes and ears so that you may understand His ways.

3. Pray for Wisdom and Understanding

James 1:5 assures us that if we lack wisdom, we should ask God, Who gives generously to all without reproach. Seek wisdom through prayer and studying God's Word.

4. Submit to God's Will

A heart that desires discernment must be willing to follow God's leading. Proverbs 9:10 says, "*The fear of the Lord is the beginning of wisdom: and the knowledge of the Holy is understanding.*" True discernment comes from a reverential fear of God and a commitment to obey His commands.

The Fruits of Discernment

When a believer walks in discernment, they experience:

- *Spiritual Maturity:* They are not easily swayed by false doctrines.
- *Righteous Living:* They choose actions that are excellent and pleasing to God.
- *Purity and Integrity:* They live sincerely, avoiding offense and remaining blameless before Christ.
- *A Fruitful Life:* Their decisions lead to Godly results, bringing glory to God.

Discernment is an essential quality that every believer must cultivate through prayer, study of the Word, and submission to the Holy Spirit. As we pray for discernment, may our love abound in wisdom and judgment so that we may walk in truth, approve what is excellent, and live blamelessly until the return of Christ.

24

PRAYER FOR DIVINE DIRECTION
(ISAIAH 30:21)

One of the greatest blessings in the Christian life is the ability to receive divine direction from God. In Isaiah 30:21, the Bible declares: *"Your ears shall hear a word behind you, saying, 'This is the way, walk in it,' whenever you turn to the right hand or whenever you turn to the left."* This promise reassures us that God desires to guide His children in every step they take. In a world full of uncertainties, confusion, and misleading voices, Divine direction is not just a privilege but a necessity for every believer.

Why Do We Need Divine Direction?

1. *To Fulfill God's Purpose:* Every believer is created with a Divine purpose (Jeremiah 29:11).

2. *To Avoid Costly Mistakes:* Many people make decisions based on emotions, pressure, or human wisdom, which often lead to unnecessary struggles. Proverbs 3:5-6 urges us to trust in the Lord and not lean on our understanding.

3. *To Walk in God's Timing:* Divine direction ensures that we move in sync with God's perfect timing. (Ecclesiastes 3:1).

4. *For Safety and Protection:* (Proverbs 14:12). God's guidance protects us from harm.

Ways God Gives Divine Direction

1. *Through His Word:* Psalm 119:105 says, *"Your Word is a lamp to my feet and a light to my path."* The Bible remains the primary source of Divine direction.

2. *Through the Holy Spirit:* The Holy Spirit dwells within us to lead and guide us into all truth (John 16:13).

3. *Through Prophetic Revelation:* God sometimes sends prophetic messages through dreams, visions, and His servants (Amos 3:7).

4. *Through Inner Witness and Peace:* The peace of God is often an indicator of His direction (Colossians 3:15).

5. *Through Circumstances and Open Doors:* Sometimes, God directs us by closing wrong doors and opening the right ones (Revelation 3:8).

Biblical Examples of Divine Direction

Abraham (Genesis 12:1-4): God called Abraham to leave his country and go to a land He would show him. Abraham obeyed and was blessed.

Moses (Exodus 3:1-12): God directed Moses through a burning bush, leading him to deliver Israel from Egypt.

Paul (Acts 16:6-10): Paul was forbidden by the Holy Spirit from preaching in Asia but was later directed to Macedonia.

Practical Steps to Seeking Divine Direction

Commit Your Plans to God in Prayer (Proverbs 16:3): Before making any decision, seek God's face.

Study and Meditate on God's Word (Joshua 1:8): The Bible provides principles that align our decisions with God's will.

Listen to the Holy Spirit (Isaiah 30:21): Be sensitive to His voice through prayer and worship.

Seek Godly Counsel (Proverbs 11:14): Wise counsel from spiritual mentors can help confirm God's direction.

Walk by Faith and Obedience (Hebrews 11:8): Once God speaks, act in faith, trusting Him for the outcome.

Prayer Points for Divine Direction

Thanksgiving: Father, thank You for the promise of divine guidance (Psalm 32:8).

Repentance: Lord, forgive me for the times I relied on my understanding instead of seeking Your direction (Proverbs 3:5-6).

Holy Spirit's Leading: Holy Spirit, lead me into all truth and order my steps in every decision I make (John 16:13).

Clarity and Discernment: Lord, open my spiritual ears to hear Your voice clearly and distinguish it from other voices (Isaiah 30:21).

Obedience to God's Will: Father, give me the grace to obey Your instructions without hesitation (Hebrews 11:8).

Closed Doors of Distraction: Lord, shut every wrong door that leads to confusion and open the right doors for me (Revelation 3:8). In Jesus' name!

Divine direction is available to every believer who seeks God diligently. It brings peace, protection, and purpose to our lives. As we develop a lifestyle of prayer, studying God's Word, and obeying His voice, we will continually walk in the path He has designed for us. Let us always remember the promise in Isaiah 30:21: *"This is the way, walk in it."*

25

PRAYER FOR UNDERSTANDING GOD'S WORD
(PSALM 119:18)

"Open my eyes, that I may behold
wondrous things out of Your law."

The Need for Spiritual Understanding

God's Word is full of treasures, yet without divine illumination, one may struggle to grasp its depth. Understanding the Scriptures goes beyond intellectual knowledge; it requires revelation from the Holy Spirit. The psalmist's prayer in Psalm 119:18 is an earnest plea for God to remove spiritual blindness and grant insight into His Divine truths.

The Bible is not just another book; it is God's voice speaking to us. Without the Holy Spirit's help, one might read but not comprehend, hear but not perceive. Jesus rebuked the Pharisees because they searched the Scriptures diligently yet they did not recognize Him as the fulfillment of God's promises (John 5:39-40). This shows that knowledge alone is insufficient; we need God to open our spiritual eyes.

How to Pray for Understanding

Ask for the Holy Spirit's Help

Jesus Christ promised that the Holy Spirit would guide us into all truth (John 16:13). When we approach the Word, we must first pray for the Spirit to enlighten our minds.

Have a Humble and Teachable Heart

God resists the proud but gives grace to the humble (James 4:6). A heart that is open and willing to learn will receive Divine revelation.

Meditate on God's Word

Joshua 1:8 instructs us to meditate on the Word day and night. Meditation allows the Holy Spirit to illuminate truths that a surface reading might not see.

Compare Scripture with Scripture

The Bible interprets itself. By studying related passages, we gain a clearer understanding of God's message.

Apply What You Learn

James 1:22 warns against being hearers only and not doers of the Word. When we put God's Word into practice, deeper understanding follows.

The Benefits of Praying for Understanding

- *Spiritual Growth:* As we grasp biblical truths, we grow in wisdom and maturity.
- *Discernment:* Understanding God's Word equips us to distinguish between truth and deception.
- *Strengthened Faith:* A deeper knowledge of Scripture strengthens our trust in God.
- *Direction in Life:* God's Word is a lamp to our feet and a light to our path (Psalm 119:105).

A Sample Prayer for Understanding

Heavenly Father, I thank You for the gift of Your Word, which is a lamp to my feet and a light to my path. I acknowledge that only with Your Spirit, I can fully understand its truths. Open my eyes, Lord, that I may behold wondrous things out of Your law. Give me a teachable heart and a hunger for Your Word. Help me not only to read but to meditate, apply, and live by Your truth. I pray for wisdom and discernment, that I may walk in Your ways. In Jesus' name, Amen.

F

PRAYERS OF FAITH AND DECLARATION

26

PRAYER OF FAITH
(MARK 11:24)

Faith is the foundation of our walk with God. The prayer of faith is a powerful tool that enables believers to access God's promises, overcome obstacles, and receive answers to their prayers. Mark 11:24 states, *"Therefore I say unto you, what things soever ye desire, when ye pray, believe that ye receive them, and ye shall have them."* This verse reveals the essence of the prayer of faith: believing that we have received our requests even before we see them manifest.

1. What is the Prayer of Faith?

The prayer of faith is a confident, unwavering petition to God based on trust in His attributes and promises. It is not a wishful hope or mere optimism but a firm assurance that God will fulfill His Word. James 5:15 says, *"And the prayer of faith shall save the sick, and the Lord shall raise him up."* This type of prayer carries authority and expectation, knowing that God is both willing and able to act.

Faith-filled prayers are grounded in:

- *God's Word:* Faith comes by hearing the Word of God (Romans 10:17). We pray based on His promises.
- *God's Attributes*: God is faithful, and He never lies (Numbers 23:19).
- *God's Power:* He is able to do exceedingly above all we ask (Ephesians 3:20).

2. Characteristics of the Prayer of Faith

A true prayer of faith has several distinguishing characteristics:

Confidence in God's Ability: Knowing that nothing is impossible for God (Luke 1:37).

Alignment with God's Will: Asking according to His will ensures that our prayers are answered (1 John 5:14-15).

Persistence in Belief: Holding onto God's promises without wavering (Hebrews 10:23).

Thanksgiving Before Manifestation: Giving thanks in advance as an act of faith (Philippians 4:6-7).

3. Biblical Examples of the Prayer of Faith

- *Elijah's Prayer for Rain (1 Kings 18:41-45)* Elijah prayed persistently, believing before he saw the rain.
- *The Woman with the Issue of Blood (Mark 5:25-34)* – She believed she would be healed if she touched Jesus' garment, and her faith made her whole.
- *Blind Bartimaeus (Mark 10:46-52)* – He cried out in faith, and Jesus granted his sight.

These examples show how faith-filled prayers lead to miraculous outcomes.

4. How to Pray the Prayer of Faith

Find a Scripture That Supports Your Request: Stand on God's Word.

Believe from Your Heart: Faith is not just spoken; it must be deeply believed.

Speak Out in Confidence: Declare your request boldly

Refuse Doubt: Reject fear and unbelief (James 1:6-7).

Give Thanks in Advance: Show gratitude as if the answer has already come.

Act on Your Faith: Faith without works is dead (James 2:17).

5. The Impact of the Prayer of Faith

The prayer of faith releases supernatural power, changes circumstances, and brings divine intervention. It strengthens our relationship with God and allows us to experience His faithfulness firsthand. When we pray in faith, we move beyond hope into certainty, seeing God's hand at work in our lives.

The prayer of faith is an essential aspect of a believer's life. As we align our prayers with God's promises, stand firm in faith, and refuse doubt, we will see His mighty hand move in our circumstances. Let us boldly approach God, believing that He hears and answers according to His perfect will.

27

PROPHETIC PRAYER AND DECREES

(ISAIAH 55:11)

"So shall My word be that goes forth from My mouth;
It shall not return to Me void,
But it shall accomplish what I please,
And it shall prosper in the thing for which I sent it."

Prophetic prayer and decrees are powerful spiritual tools that believers can use to align their lives with God's will. These are prayers that declare God's purposes, enforce His Word, and bring divine realities into manifestation. Through prophetic declarations, believers speak forth God's Word, His promises with faith, into existence.

Understanding Prophetic Prayer

Prophetic prayer is praying with divine insight, inspired by the Holy Spirit. It involves perceiving God's will for a situation and speaking it into reality. This kind of prayer is based on faith in

God's revealed Word and the leading of the Holy Spirit. It is more than supplication; it is an authoritative release of divine power.

Key Aspects of Prophetic Prayer:

1. *Hearing from God:* Effective prophetic prayer begins with hearing from God. Whether through Scripture, dreams, visions, or inner promptings, believers must be attuned to God's voice.

2. *Speaking with Authority:* When we pray prophetically, we do not ask; we declare and enforce the will of God in the spiritual realm.

3. *Aligning with God's Word:* Prophetic prayer is not based on human desires but on the revealed truth of Scripture. It is declaring God's promises with faith.

4. *Persistence and Boldness:* Prophetic prayer requires boldness to decree God's Word over circumstances and persistence to see the manifestation.

The Power of Decrees

Decrees are authoritative statements made in agreement with God's Word to establish His will on earth. Isaiah 55:11 reminds us that when God's Word is spoken, it will not return void; it will fulfill its divine assignment.

Why Are Decrees Powerful?

- *They Activate God's Promises:* When believers decree God's Word, they set spiritual laws in motion that bring divine fulfillment.

- *They Shift Circumstances:* Prophetic decrees can change impossible situations, bringing healing, deliverance, and breakthrough.
- *They Silence the Enemy:* satan likes lies and deception, but decrees of truth dismantle his plans.
- *They Accomplish Divine Purpose:* As Isaiah 55:11 assures, God's Word prospers in the very thing it was sent to do; when we decree His Word, it carries His authority.

Biblical Examples of Prophetic Declarations

1. *Ezekiel Prophesying to Dry Bones:* Ezekiel was commanded to prophesy life into dry bones, and they lived (Ezekiel 37:4-10).
2. *Jesus Commanding the Storm:* Jesus Christ spoke, "Peace, be still," and the storm ceased (Mark 4:39).
3. *Apostolic Declarations:* Peter and John declared healing to the lame man, saying, "In the name of Jesus Christ of Nazareth, rise up and walk" (Acts 3:6).

How to Make Prophetic Decrees

Identify a Biblical Promise: Search the Scriptures for God's promises concerning your situation.

Personalize the Scripture: Speak it as a personal declaration, e.g., "By His stripes, I am healed" (Isaiah 53:5).

Declare with Faith: Speak boldly, believing that God will establish your words.

Remain Consistent: Continually declare God's Word until you see results.

Give Thanks: Praise God in advance for the fulfillment of His Word.

Sample Prophetic Decrees

- *For Healing:* "I decree and declare that by the stripes of Jesus Christ, I am healed and whole (Isaiah 53:5)."
- *For Provision:* "The Lord shall supply all my needs according to His riches in glory by Christ Jesus (Philippians 4:19)."
- *For Deliverance:* "No weapon formed against me shall prosper; every tongue that rises against me in judgment, I condemn (Isaiah 54:17)."
- *For Spiritual Growth:* "I am growing in the grace and knowledge of the Lord Jesus Christ (2 Peter 3:18)."

Prophetic prayer and decrees are powerful tools for enforcing God's will in our lives. As believers, we must align our words with Scripture, speaking life and divine purpose over our situations. When we declare God's Word in faith, it will not return void; it will prosper and fulfill God's intended purpose. Let us rise with boldness, declaring and decreeing the purposes of God over our lives, families, churches, and nations. Amen!

28

PRAYER OF AGREEMENT
(MATTHEW 18:19)

The Prayer of Agreement is a powerful biblical principle that Jesus Christ taught us. In Matthew 18:19, Jesus said, *"Again I say to you that if two of you agree on earth concerning anything that they ask, it will be done for them by My Father in heaven."* This form of prayer brings believers together in unity, allowing them to stand in faith for God's will to be manifested.

The Power of Unity in Prayer

God places great emphasis on unity. Psalm 133:1 declares, *"Behold, how good and how pleasant it is for brethren to dwell together in unity!"* When believers come together in one accord, their prayers become more effective. The early Church practiced this form of prayer, as seen in Acts 1:14: *"These all continued with one accord in prayer and supplication."*

When two or more people come into agreement, their prayers have divine backing. Agreement in prayer is not just a verbal consent but involves unity in faith, spirit, and expectation. This kind of prayer is particularly effective for situations requiring divine intervention, such as healing, provision, deliverance, or revival.

Keys to Effective Prayer of Agreement

1. *Unity in Faith:* Those praying together must genuinely believe that God will answer their prayer. James 1:6 warns against doubting, saying, *"But let him ask in faith, with no doubting, for he who doubts is like a wave of the sea driven and tossed by the wind."*

2. *Agreement on the Specific Request:* Those involved must have a clear, unified petition before God. Amos 3:3 asks, *"Can two walk together, unless they are agreed?"*

3. *Standing on God's Word:* Agreement should be based on scriptural promises. Praying according to God's Word ensures alignment with His will (1 John 5:14-15).

4. *Persistence in Prayer:* Agreement means believers must continue in prayer until they all see the manifestation of answers (Luke 18:1-8).

5. *Confession and Thanksgiving:* Declaring God's promises and giving thanks in advance strengthens faith (Philippians 4:6-7).

Biblical Examples of the Prayer of Agreement

- *The Disciples in the Upper Room* (Acts 2:1-4): Before Pentecost, the disciples were *"in one accord in one place."* The Holy Spirit descended powerfully because of their unified prayer.

- *Peter's Release from Prison* (Acts 12:5-12): The Church earnestly prayed together for Peter, and an angel delivered him miraculously.

- *Jehoshaphat and Judah* (2 Chronicles 20:3-22): Facing a vast enemy army, Jehoshaphat led Judah in prayer and fasting. They stood together, and God granted them victory.

How to Apply the Prayer of Agreement

1. *Find a Faith Partner:* This could be a spouse, friend, pastor, or prayer group that shares your faith and belief in God's promises.

2. *Clearly Define the Request:* Ensure that all involved fully understand and agree on what they are asking God for.

3. *Pray Together Aloud:* Speaking the request in unity increases spiritual focus and agreement.

4. *Continue in Faith:* Maintain faith and stand firm on God's promises.

5. *Give Thanks:* Thank God for the answer in advance, demonstrating trust in His faithfulness.

The Prayer of Agreement is a divine strategy given by Jesus Christ to unlock supernatural breakthroughs. It brings unity in the Body of Christ and strengthens faith among believers. As we come together in agreement, aligning our prayers with God's will, we position ourselves to receive powerful answers from heaven.

29

PRAYER OF BOLD CONFESSION
(ROMANS 10:10)

"For with the heart one believes unto righteousness,
and with the mouth confession is made unto salvation."

The Power of Bold Confession

Confession is a powerful principle in the Christian faith. It is not only speaking words but declaring the truth of God's Word with faith. Romans 10:10 reveals that believing in the heart leads to righteousness, but confession with the mouth brings about salvation. This truth extends salvation to every area of our lives; healing, deliverance, victory, and spiritual breakthroughs.

A bold confession is a statement of faith based on God's promises, spoken with full conviction, regardless of circumstances. It aligns our speech with God's will, activating His power in our lives.

Biblical Examples of Bold Confession

1. *David before Goliath* (*1 Samuel 17:45-47*): David did not just believe in his heart that God would give him victory; he boldly confessed it before facing the giant. His words reflected his confidence in God, and his confession preceded his triumph.

2. *The Woman with the Issue of Blood* (*Mark 5:28*) She kept saying, "*If only I may touch His clothes, I shall be made well.*" Her confession of faith led to her healing.

Why Bold Confession is Necessary

It Aligns us with God's Word: When we confess what God says, we bring our hearts, minds, and circumstances in agreement with His will.

It Activates Faith: Faith is released through words. As we declare God's promises, faith rises within us, and we receive what we believe.

It Counters the Enemy's Lies: The devil seeks to fill believers with fear, doubt, and discouragement. Bold confession declares God's truth in the face of opposition.

It Brings Manifestation: Confessing God's Word persistently brings results.

How to Practice Bold Confession

1. *Identify God's Promises:* Search the Scriptures for God's promises concerning your need (e.g., healing, provision, strength).

2. *Believe in Your Heart:* Meditate on the Word until it is firmly rooted in your spirit.

3. *Speak Aloud with Confidence:* Declare the Word of God over your life daily. Speak as if it is already done.

4. *Stay Persistent:* Do not stop confessing even when circumstances seem unchanged. Keep declaring until manifestation comes.

5. *Refuse to Speak Contrary Words:* Do not nullify your confession by speaking doubt, fear, or unbelief.

Scriptural Confessions for Bold Confession

For Salvation: "I confess Jesus as my Lord and Savior. I believe in my heart that God raised Him from the dead. I am saved." (Romans 10:9-10)

For Strength: "The Lord is the Strength of my life; I will not fear." (Psalm 27:1)

For Healing: "By His stripes, I am healed." (Isaiah 53:5)

For Provision: "My God shall supply all my needs according to His riches in glory by Christ Jesus." (Philippians 4:19)

For Victory: "Thanks be to God, who gives me the victory through our Lord Jesus Christ." (1 Corinthians 15:57)

A prayer of bold confession is not wishful thinking; it is faith in action. As we align our words with God's promises and speak with unwavering confidence, we activate divine power in our lives. Let your confession be bold, unwavering, and full of faith, and watch God's promises come to pass in your life!

30

PRAYER FOR STRENGTHENING FAITH
(LUKE 22:32)

Faith is the cornerstone of the Christian life. It is the bedrock on which we build our relationship with God and experience His power. Without faith, it is impossible to please God (Hebrews 11:6), and it is through faith that we are able to receive God's promises. However, there are times in every believer's life when faith is challenged. In these moments, prayer for the strengthening of faith becomes crucial. One of the most poignant passages on this topic is found in Luke 22:32, where Jesus Christ prays for Peter's faith, stating, *"But I have prayed for you, Simon, that your faith may not fail. And when you have turned back, strengthen your brothers."*

The Context of Luke 22:32

In this powerful moment, Jesus is speaking to Simon Peter just before His arrest. He knows that Peter is about to face one of the greatest challenges of his life: the temptation to deny Jesus. Despite Peter's confidence that he would never betray Jesus, Jesus, in His perfect knowledge, foresees Peter's reaction. Jesus does not condemn Peter but Christ prays for him a prayer for his faith. He prays that Peter's faith may not fail, knowing that this period of trial would ultimately lead to Peter's restoration and strengthening. Afterward, Peter would be able to encourage and strengthen his brothers.

The Importance of Strengthening Faith

Faith is not a passive belief, but an active reliance on God's promises, His Word, and His power. Strengthening faith involves cultivating a deeper trust in God's sovereignty and goodness, especially when circumstances challenge our understanding.

1. Faith Strengthened Through Trials:

James 1:2-4 teaches us that trials and difficulties are an opportunity for our faith to be tested and strengthened. "Consider it pure joy, my brothers and sisters, whenever you face trials of many kinds, because you know that the testing of your faith produces perseverance. Let perseverance finish its work so that you may be mature and complete, not lacking anything." Here, we see that trials are not a sign of God's abandonment but an opportunity for growth. Our faith becomes stronger as we learn to rely more fully on God during hardships.

2. Faith Strengthened Through Prayer:

The power of prayer cannot be underestimated in the process of strengthening faith. When we pray, we acknowledge our dependence on God and invite Him to work in our hearts. Prayer is a conduit through which the Holy Spirit helps us grow in faith. Luke 22:32 emphasizes that Jesus prays for Peter, and in the same way, we can ask Jesus to intercede on our behalf, just as He did for Peter. Through prayer, we receive the strength to endure challenges and to believe that God is faithful, even when we cannot see the full picture.

3. Faith Strengthened Through the Word of God:

Romans 10:17 tells us, "So then faith comes by hearing, and hearing by the word of God." The Word of God is the ultimate source of faith. By meditating on Scripture, we are reminded of God's promises, His past faithfulness, and His ability to bring us through every situation. As we read the Bible and internalize its truth, our faith is nurtured and fortified. We must make time daily to read and meditate on God's Word, allowing it to dwell richly in our hearts.

4. Faith Strengthened Through Fellowship:

In the body of Christ, believers are called to strengthen one another in their faith. Hebrews 10:24-25 encourages us to "consider how we may spur one another on toward love and good deeds, not giving up meeting together... but encouraging one another." Just as Jesus prayed for Peter, we too are called to pray for one another, especially when someone's faith is faltering. Fellowship with other believers provides an opportunity for mutual support, accountability, and encouragement. As we encourage others, our own faith is strengthened.

Prayer for Strengthening Faith

A key aspect of strengthening faith is prayer. Jesus' prayer for Peter reveals a few vital points that we can incorporate into our own prayers:

- *Recognition of Weakness*: We begin by acknowledging our weakness. Just as Peter was unaware of his impending denial, we often don't fully recognize our need for faith until we are in the midst of a trial. Jesus' prayer for Peter was not about condemnation but about recognizing that we are weak and in need of God's help. In our prayers, we should be honest about our struggles and our doubts.

- *Intercession of Jesus*: Jesus interceded for Peter, and we are reminded that we have a high priest in heaven who is continually praying for us (Romans 8:34). Our prayers for strengthening faith should be an act of surrender, asking Jesus to intercede on our behalf, especially during times of trial. We can also ask the Holy Spirit to help us in our weakness (Romans 8:26-27).

- *Purpose in Trials*: Jesus' prayer also reveals that our trials are not meaningless. When we pray for strengthening faith, we must recognize that God allows challenges in our lives for a purpose. These trials are not to defeat us but to refine us. They produce perseverance, character, and hope (Romans 5:3-5). We can pray that God would help us see the purpose in our suffering and remain faithful in the midst of it.

A Sample Prayer for Strengthening Faith

Heavenly Father,

Thank You for Your love and care. I come before You today, acknowledging my weaknesses and my need for Your help. I know that in my own strength, I cannot endure the challenges I face, but I trust in Your ability to strengthen my faith. Just as You prayed for Peter, I ask that You pray for me, that my faith may not fail.

Strengthen my trust in You, even when I cannot understand my circumstances. Help me to rely on Your promises, knowing that You are faithful. Renew my heart with hope and perseverance, and help me to grow in faith through every trial.

Thank You for the power of Your Word, the encouragement of fellow believers, and the intercession of Jesus. I surrender my doubts and fears to You, knowing that You are with me and will never leave me.

In Jesus' name, I pray. Amen.

Strengthening our faith is a lifelong process, one that requires intentionality, perseverance, and prayer. Just as Jesus prayed for Peter's faith, we too can seek God's help in strengthening our faith, particularly during times of trial and difficulty. As we turn to God in prayer, seek His Word, and rely on the support of the body of Christ, our faith will be strengthened, and we will emerge from our trials more steadfast and more mature in our walk with God. Let us continue to pray for one another, strengthening the faith of the body of Christ, and holding onto the promises of God, knowing that He is faithful to complete the work He has begun in us.

G

PRAYERS OF
REPENTANCE AND
CLEANSING

31

PRAYER OF REPENTANCE
(PSALM 51:1-2)

Repentance is a fundamental aspect of the Christian faith, necessary for restoring our relationship with God whenever sin has crept in. The Prayer of Repentance in **Psalm 51:1-2** gives us a powerful model to follow when seeking God's forgiveness. Psalm 51 is attributed to David after his transgression with Bathsheba. This psalm serves as a heartfelt cry to God for mercy, healing, and cleansing, and it continues to resonate with believers today. It invites us to approach God with a broken and contrite heart, asking for restoration and renewal.

1. Understanding the Psalm 51:1-2 Prayer

Psalm 51:1-2 says:

"Have mercy upon me, O God,
According to Your lovingkindness;
According to the multitude of Your tender mercies,
Blot out my transgressions.
Wash me thoroughly from my iniquity,
And cleanse me from my sin."

This prayer begins with a plea for mercy. David acknowledges God's goodness and tender compassion, recognizing that forgiveness and cleansing come only from God. In these verses, David sets the tone for the entire psalm, focusing on God' and expressing his deep need for grace and mercy.

2. The Importance of Repentance

Repentance means turning away from sin and turning toward God. It is not just about feeling remorse for the wrong done, but also about making a conscious decision to change. The Prayer of Repentance is a declaration of humility, recognizing our brokenness and need for God's mercy. The need to address our sin before God, confessing it and seeking His forgiveness.

Repentance also allows us to experience spiritual healing and renewal. When we confess our sins and receive forgiveness, we can walk in freedom and righteousness once again. The Prayer of Repentance in Psalm 51 exemplifies this process; acknowledging sin, pleading for mercy, and asking for a cleansing of the soul.

3. Components of the Prayer of Repentance

Plea for Mercy (Psalm 51:1)

David starts by appealing to God's mercy. He asks for mercy *"according to Your lovingkindness"* and *"the multitude of Your tender mercies."* By invoking God's mercy, David is acknowledging that forgiveness is a gift, not something earned. The mercy of God is not based on our deserving, but on God's unmerited grace and love for us.

Blotting Out Transgressions (Psalm 51:1)

To *"blot out"* means to erase or completely remove. David asks God to blot out his transgressions, symbolizing the complete removal of sin from his record. This shows that God has the power to erase our sins, no matter how great they may be. Repentance allows for a fresh start with God, where our sins are remembered no more.

Washing from Iniquity (Psalm 51:2)

David uses the imagery of washing to describe the purification process, because sin stains, making someone spiritually unclean, and only God can cleanse us. The act of washing is symbolic of the inner transformation that takes place when we seek forgiveness through repentance. The cleansing power of God's grace washes away the guilt, shame, and filth of sin.

Cleansing from sin (Psalm 51:2)

David asks God to cleanse him from sin. It not only affects our actions but also our hearts and minds. God's cleansing brings a deep, inner renewal that restores the sinner to a right relationship with Him. Cleansing is an ongoing process in the life of a believer, as we continue to grow and mature in our faith.

4. The Role of the Heart in Repentance

A true Prayer of Repentance goes beyond words. It must come from a sincere heart. David's heart was deeply convicted of his sin, and this prompted him to call out to God. True repentance involves more than confessing sin; it requires a willingness to change and a desire to turn away from the sinful behavior that led to separation from God.

Repentance should be heartfelt. It is not about going through the motions but expressing genuine sorrow for sins and a desire for restoration. When we approach God with a broken heart, He is faithful to forgive and restore.

5. The Fruits of Repentance

The Prayer of Repentance in Psalm 51 is not only a plea for forgiveness but also a recognition of the need for transformation. True repentance leads to change. After David prays for forgiveness and cleansing, he goes on to ask God to *"create in me a clean heart"* (Psalm 51:10). This demonstrates that repentance brings forth a desire for inner renewal and purity, resulting in a heart that seeks to follow God's will.

Repentance also enables us to forgive others. Jesus taught us to forgive others as we have been forgiven. The Prayer of Repentance helps us walk in the freedom that comes from God's forgiveness, and it allows us to extend that same forgiveness to others.

6. Applying the Prayer of Repentance Today

We can learn from David's prayer and apply it to our own lives. When we sin, we are called to immediately come before God, acknowledging our wrongs, asking for forgiveness, and seeking His cleansing. The Prayer of Repentance is a model we can follow in our personal prayer time. It helps us understand that repentance is not only for the "big" sins but also for the smaller moments where we may have fallen short in our thoughts, attitudes, or actions.

We must also remember that repentance is a lifestyle. It is not something that happens only when we've made major mistakes. Rather, it is part of our ongoing relationship with God, helping us to stay close to Him and grow in holiness.

The Prayer of Repentance in Psalm 51:1-2 is a powerful example of how to approach God when we recognize our need for forgiveness and restoration. It teaches us to appeal for God's mercy, to ask for the cleansing of our hearts, and to seek renewal from within. Through repentance, we experience God's grace and are restored to a right relationship with Him.

As believers, we should regularly incorporate repentance into our prayer lives, acknowledging our sins and seeking God's forgiveness. May this psalm inspire us to approach God with humility and sincerity, trusting in His boundless mercy and love.

32

PRAYER OF CONFESSION
(1 JOHN 1:9)

The prayer of confession is one of the most powerful and freeing forms of prayer. It is the means by which we acknowledge our sins before God, repent, and experience His forgiveness and cleansing.

In 1 John 1:9, we are given a clear promise: *"If we confess our sins, He is faithful and just to forgive us our sins and to cleanse us from all unrighteousness."* This verse is a reminder that confession is not just about admitting wrongdoings but about experiencing the transformative power of God's forgiveness and cleansing.

Understanding Confession

Confession, in the context of prayer, goes beyond admitting sin. It involves recognizing our wrongdoings, taking full responsibility for them, and agreeing with God about the gravity of our sin. It is not an attempt to minimize or justify our actions but to be honest before God, acknowledging that our sins have separated us from Him. This act of confession brings us to a place of humility and repentance, enabling us to receive God's mercy.

The Greek word for confession, *homologeo*, means "to say the same thing as" or "to agree with." When we confess our sins, we are agreeing with God that what we have done is wrong and that we need His forgiveness. It is a declaration that we are ready to turn away from sin and back to God.

The Faithfulness of God (1 John 1:9)

1 John 1:9 emphasizes the faithfulness of God in forgiving and cleansing us. The verse tells us that God is *"faithful and just"* to forgive our sins. God's faithfulness is a cornerstone of His character. He never breaks His promises, and He promises to forgive us when we come to Him in confession. This promise is not based on our worthiness but on God's steadfast love and grace.

It's important to understand that God's forgiveness is not conditional upon our perfection or ability to "make up" for our sins. His forgiveness is grounded in the finished work of Jesus Christ on the cross. Jesus took the punishment for our sins, and because of His sacrifice, we can approach God with confidence, knowing that He will forgive us when we confess.

Cleansing from All Unrighteousness

Along with forgiveness, God promises to cleanse us *"from all unrighteousness."* This cleansing goes beyond simply wiping the slate clean. It signifies a deep spiritual renewal, where God removes the guilt, and stain of sin. His cleansing is thorough and complete, transforming us from the inside out. It is an act of sanctification, where God purifies us and restores our fellowship with Him.

The cleansing from unrighteousness also has a practical aspect. When we confess our sins, we open ourselves to the work of the Holy Spirit, who empowers us to overcome sin and live a life of righteousness. True confession leads to transformation as we submit to God's work in our hearts, allowing His grace to empower us to live according to His will.

The Importance of Regular Confession

The prayer of confession should not be seen as a one-time event but as a regular part of our Christian walk. Regular confession keeps our hearts aligned with God and helps us maintain a clear conscience before Him. It is a way to ensure that we are continually growing in our relationship with God, removing any barriers that might hinder our fellowship with Him.

The practice of daily or frequent confession also helps us stay humble, reminding us of our dependence on God's grace. It prevents us from becoming self-righteous or prideful, recognizing that we all need God's mercy every day. It keeps us open to the conviction of the Holy Spirit and sensitive to the areas in our lives that need to be surrendered to God.

The Role of Repentance

Confession and repentance go hand in hand. While confession is about acknowledging our sin, repentance is about turning away from it. The prayer of confession should always be accompanied by a heart of repentance. Repentance is a change of mind and direction. It is not enough to simply confess our sins; we must also make the intentional decision to turn away from them and to follow God's ways.

In the New Testament, repentance is closely tied to faith in Jesus Christ. When we confess our sins, we are called to repent, turning to Jesus as our Savior and Lord. Repentance is a vital part of the process of restoration, allowing us to experience the fullness of God's forgiveness and cleansing. It is not just about feeling sorry for our sins, but about a complete change of heart and direction that leads to a transformed life.

Practical Steps in the Prayer of Confession

1. *Acknowledge your sins:* Take time to reflect on the areas where you have fallen short of God's standards. Ask the Holy Spirit to reveal any hidden sins or areas of your life that need to be surrendered to Him.

2. *Agree with God about your sin:* Confession is about agreeing with God that sin is wrong. Do not try to justify or downplay your sin. Acknowledge it for what it is and express your desire to turn away from it.

3. *Ask for forgiveness:* In your prayer, ask God to forgive you. Trust in His promise that He is faithful and just to forgive you.

4. *Repent:* Make a conscious decision to turn away from sin and change your behavior. This may involve seeking accountability, making restitution, and taking steps to avoid the temptation in the future.

5. *Receive God's forgiveness:* Believe that God has forgiven you and that He has cleansed you from all unrighteousness. Walk in the freedom that comes from His grace.

The prayer of confession is not just about seeking forgiveness but about experiencing the transformative power of God's grace. It is an opportunity for us to align our hearts with God, receive His forgiveness, and be cleansed from sin. When we approach God in confession, we are reminded of His faithfulness, justice, and mercy. Through confession, we are restored to right fellowship with God, empowered by His grace to live according to His will.

As you engage in the prayer of confession, remember that God's forgiveness is always available to those who humbly seek it. Trust in His promises and allow His cleansing work to transform your life. Let the prayer of confession be a daily practice that draws you closer to God, strengthens your faith, and empowers you to live in the freedom God offers.

33

PRAYER FOR HEART CLEANSING
(PSALM 139:23-24)

Introduction to Heart Cleansing Prayer

In the journey of faith, the heart plays a big role. The heart is the center of our desires, thoughts, intentions, and actions. It is where our motivations are birthed. As believers, we are called to maintain a pure heart before God, one that reflects His nature and purpose. This makes the prayer for heart cleansing essential in our daily walk with Him.

In Psalm 139:23-24, David prays:

Search me, O God, and know my heart;
Try me, and know my anxieties;
24 And see if there is any wicked way in me,
And lead me in the way everlasting.

This heartfelt prayer is an invitation to God to inspect and purify our inner selves. David's plea for a heart cleansing is not only an acknowledgment of his own limitations but also a deep desire for

God's transforming work in his life. This prayer is one we should model in our own lives, asking God to search our hearts, reveal any hidden sin, and guide us towards righteousness.

The Importance of Heart Cleansing

The Bible speaks extensively about the heart and its influence on our lives. Proverbs 4:23 tells us:

"Keep your heart with all diligence,
For out of it spring the issues of life."

The condition of our hearts directly impacts our thoughts, words, and actions. A heart that is not purified can harbor bitterness, anger, unforgiveness, pride, and many other emotions that are contrary to God's will.

Jesus Christ our Lord emphasized the importance of a pure heart in His Sermon.

In Matthew 5:8, He said,

"Blessed are the pure in heart,
For they shall see God."

This statement shows the spiritual truth that a heart that is cleansed by God is essential for a deeper relationship with Him. It allows us to reflect His character and be vessels of His love and grace.

When we pray for heart cleansing, we are asking God to remove everything that hinders our communion with Him and to restore us to a state of purity that aligns with His holiness. This prayer involves an openness to His examination and correction, allowing God to deal with areas of our lives that we may not even be aware of.

The Power of God's Searchlight

Psalm 139:23 begins with a bold request: *"Search me, O God, and know my heart."* This is an invitation for God to examine every part of us. The word "search" suggests an intentional, thorough inspection; nothing is hidden from God's sight. He knows our deepest thoughts, motivations, and desires, even those we may try to conceal from ourselves.

This request reflects an understanding that God's perspective is perfect. While we may deceive ourselves or rationalize our actions, God sees the truth. The apostle Paul writes in Hebrews 4:13:

"And there is no creature hidden from His sight, but all things are naked and open to the eyes of Him to whom we must give account."

When we open ourselves up to God's searchlight, we invite Him to reveal areas in our hearts that need His touch.

God's search is not meant to condemn us but to purify us. As we invite God to reveal hidden motives, we are also asking Him to cleanse us from any unrighteousness. His conviction leads to our transformation, and His grace empowers us to walk in holiness.

Testing the Heart: A Prayer for Purity

In the second part of Psalm 139:23, David prays, *"Test me and know my anxious thoughts."* Testing involves a process of refinement, much like gold being refined in the fire. When we ask

God to test us, we are asking Him to evaluate the motives of our hearts, to reveal what is pure and what is impure.

Anxiety and fear often take root in the hearts, especially when one is not trusting fully in God. Anxiety can cloud the judgment and distort the ability to discern God's will. Through the prayer of heart cleansing, we ask God to examine our hearts, our thoughts and remove anything that is contrary to His peace.

It is important to note that God's testing is not for punishment but for purification.

Seeing the Offensive Ways in Us

David continues in verse 24 with the prayer, *"And see if there is any wicked way in me."* As humans, one can sometimes be blind to his own sin. However, God's standard of holiness is different. He does not measure sin by human standards but by His perfect righteousness. When we pray for God to reveal any offensive way in us, we are asking Him to shine His light on any areas of disobedience, pride, or selfishness that hinder our relationship with Him and with others.

This prayer requires humility, as it acknowledges that we may not always be aware of the sin in our hearts. It is a surrendering of our pride and a willingness to be corrected by God.

Leading us in the Way Everlasting

David concludes his prayer with a request for God to *"lead me in the way everlasting."* The ultimate goal of heart cleansing is to align our hearts with God's will and walk in the path He has prepared for us. The "way everlasting" refers to the eternal way of righteousness, the path that leads to God's presence and reflects His character in our lives.

When we ask God to lead us in this way, we are expressing a desire to live according to His commands and to be transformed into His likeness. It is a prayer for direction and guidance in every aspect of our lives, from our thoughts and attitudes to our actions and relationships.

This prayer also points to the eternal nature of God's work in us. Heart cleansing is not a one-time event but a continuous process of sanctification. As we walk with God, He continually refines us, making us more like Christ each day.

The prayer for heart cleansing is one of the most powerful prayers we can pray as believers. It invites God to examine, test, and purify our hearts, revealing any sin or impurities that need to be dealt with. This prayer is not only about personal transformation but also about drawing closer to God and reflecting His love, peace, and righteousness to the world around us.

As we pray Psalm 139:23-24, let us be open to God's examination and correction. Let us surrender our hearts to His refining work, trusting that He will lead us in the way everlasting. May this prayer be a regular part of our spiritual lives, as we seek to live in purity and alignment with God's will.

34

PRAYER FOR DELIVERANCE FROM SIN
(JOHN 8:36)

"Therefore if the Son makes you free,
you shall be free indeed."

The power of sin can enslave a person; binding the mind, weakening the will, and corrupting the heart. But the good news of the gospel is that Jesus Christ not only forgives sin; He **delivers** us from its dominion. Deliverance from sin is more than forgiveness; it is the breaking of the chains that keep one returning to the same destructive habits, thoughts, and behaviors.

Jesus didn't come only to cover sin but to destroy its power. As the Scripture declares, *"For this purpose the Son of God was manifested, that He might destroy the works of the devil"* 1 John 3:8.

Sin is one of the devil's greatest works in humanity, and Christ came to set us free from it.

This chapter explores how to pray for true deliverance from sin and experience freedom that lasts.

2. Jesus Breaks the Chains

In John 8:34, 36 Jesus said:

"Most assuredly, I say to you, whoever commits sin is a slave of sin."

He was not speaking of a single act of sin but a **pattern**, a lifestyle that dominates the person. A slave has no control over their own life, and so it is with someone bound by sin. But Jesus continued in verse 36:

"Therefore if the Son makes you free, you shall be free indeed."

This freedom is real, total, and irreversible when received in full. It is not just the cancellation of guilt, it is **deliverance from bondage**. You don't have to live in defeat. There is power in the name of Jesus to break every chain.

3. The Role of Prayer in Deliverance

Deliverance begins when one acknowledges the struggle, surrenders his heart to God, and cry out in faith. True prayer for deliverance from sin goes beyond saying "sorry." It is an act of **warfare**. It's a confrontation with spiritual powers and the sinful nature. Prayer activates God's grace and power to sever ties with sin.

Psalm 32:5 says:

"I acknowledged my sin to You, and my iniquity I have not hidden. I said, 'I will confess my transgressions to the Lord,' and You forgave the iniquity of my sin."

That is the beginning. But deliverance comes when we walk daily in the power of the Spirit and continually pray as Jesus taught in the Lord's Prayer:

"And do not lead us into temptation, but deliver us from the evil one." (Matthew 6:13)

This prayer is not passive; it is a cry for active intervention from God to rescue us from the trap of sin.

4. Walking in the Spirit: The Pathway to Freedom

Deliverance from sin is not a one-time event but a lifestyle of dependence on the Holy Spirit. The Bible says:

"Walk in the Spirit, and you shall not fulfill the lust of the flesh." (Galatians 5:16)

When we invite the Holy Spirit to lead us daily through prayer, worship, and obedience, He empowers us to say "no" to sin and "yes" to righteousness. Deliverance is maintained by choosing the Spirit over the flesh moment by moment.

Romans 8:2 gives us this assurance:

"For the law of the Spirit of life in Christ Jesus has made me free from the law of sin and death."

What used to rule you no longer has legal power when you are under the authority of Jesus.

5. A Prayer for Deliverance from Sin

Heavenly Father,

I come to You in the mighty name of Jesus Christ. I thank You for the victory that is in the cross and the power of the blood of Jesus. Your Word says that if the Son sets me free, I shall be free indeed. Lord, I confess that I cannot free myself from this sin but You are my Deliverer.

I renounce every hidden sin, every secret habit, every stronghold that is not of You. I break agreement with the lies of the enemy and declare that I am no longer a slave to sin, but a child of God. By the authority of Jesus Christ, I command every chain to be broken: every addiction, every pattern, every lust, every deception.

Holy Spirit, come and fill me afresh. Empower me to walk in purity, in truth, and in freedom. Teach me to love righteousness and hate iniquity. I receive Your grace and choose to walk in the Spirit.

Thank You, Lord, for hearing my cry and delivering me. I stand on Your Word and declare my freedom. In Jesus' name. **Amen.**

Deliverance from sin is possible. You are not called to live in constant defeat. Through the blood of Jesus, the power of the Holy Spirit, and consistent, honest prayer, **you can walk in victory.** Cry out to God; not just to forgive, but to deliver. He is mighty to save.

Let this be your declaration today:

"Sin shall not have dominion over me, for I am not under law but under grace." Romans 6:14

There is freedom for you. Walk in it.

35

PRAYER OF REDEDICATION TO GOD
(ROMANS 12:1)

The Prayer of Rededication is a powerful act of recommitting oneself to God, acknowledging His sovereignty and grace, and seeking His will above all else. This prayer stems from the call in Romans 12:1, where Paul urges believers to offer their bodies as living sacrifices, holy and pleasing to God, as this is their true and proper worship.

"I beseech you therefore, brethren, by the mercies of God, that you present your bodies a living sacrifice, holy, acceptable to God, which is your reasonable service." Romans 12:1

In this verse, Paul provides a clear call to rededicate our lives to God. We are urged to present ourselves to God not as passive beings but as living sacrifices, consciously choosing to live according to His will. This act of rededication goes beyond just words; it involves a transformation of the heart, mind, and actions, aligning them with God's perfect purposes for our lives.

The key to understanding rededication is recognizing God's mercy. It is His mercy that makes it possible for us to come before Him, no longer separated by sin but brought near by the blood of Jesus Christ. Our rededication is not an attempt to earn God's favor; rather, it is a response to His incredible love and grace.

When we rededicate ourselves to God, we are acknowledging His complete Lordship over our lives. We are saying, "Lord, everything I am, everything I have, belongs to You." This commitment requires a deliberate act of surrender, which means we are choosing to lay down our own desires, ambitions, and plans in exchange for God's perfect will. In doing so, we trust that He knows what is best for us and will guide our paths according to His purpose.

Let's break down the elements of Romans 12:1:

"I beseech you therefore, brethren…"

Paul's plea comes from a deep sense of urgency. The word "beseech " here is more than a gentle suggestion; it is a call to action, a call that requires a response. The appeal is not to simply agree with the idea of rededication, but to actively participate in it.

"By the mercies of God…"

Our rededication is not based on our efforts or worthiness but on God's mercy. It is His mercy that enables us to approach Him and offer ourselves to Him. This perspective shifts the focus from self-reliance to total dependence on God's grace.

"That you present your bodies a living sacrifice…"

A sacrifice implies that something is given up. To offer our bodies as a living sacrifice. We are called to live our lives fully for God, in every aspect; our time, energy, talents, and resources.

Rededication is also about holiness. Paul speaks of presenting our bodies as *"holy, acceptable to God."* This means living a life set apart for God's purposes. It's about intentionality, choosing to live according to God's standards, rather than the world's. Holiness is not an isolated act but a lifestyle that flows from the heart's desire to please God.

Furthermore, the prayer of rededication is about **worship.** *"Which is your reasonable service."* This shifts our understanding of worship from something that happens once in a while to a way of life. Worship is how we live out our devotion to God daily. When we rededicate ourselves to God, every moment becomes an opportunity for worship.

In this light, rededication is not a one-time event but a continuous journey of surrender and renewal. It is a daily decision to live for God, offering our lives as instruments of righteousness.

Steps to Praying the Prayer of Rededication

Acknowledge God's Mercy

Begin by meditating on God's mercy. Reflect on His grace in your life; the forgiveness He has extended to you, the love He continually shows, and His unending faithfulness. Praise Him for His goodness.

Surrender Yourself

Confess that you are a living sacrifice. Offer yourself completely to God: your body, your heart, your mind, your will, and your emotions. This surrender may involve letting go of things you have been holding on to, whether they are sinful habits, self-centered desires, or plans that do not align with God's will.

Commit to Holiness

Ask God to help you live a life that is holy and pleasing to Him. Surrender your desires, your relationships, and your actions to His will. Invite the Holy Spirit to help you live in God's holiness in your daily life.

Renew Your Mind

The process of rededication involves not just the external but also the internal transformation. Romans 12:2 speaks of the renewal of the mind. Ask God to renew your thinking, to transform the way you see yourself, the world, and His purposes for you.

Seek to Worship in Every Area

Commit to seeing every part of your life as an act of worship. Whether in your work, relationships, or personal moments, seek to glorify God in all things. Your rededication should be evident in how you live, not just what you say.

A Sample Prayer of Rededication

Heavenly Father,

I come before You today with a heart full of gratitude for Your mercy and grace. I thank You for sending Your Son, Jesus, to save me and for bringing me near to You despite my shortcomings. Today, I choose to rededicate my life to You. I offer myself to You as a living sacrifice; holy and pleasing in Your sight.

I surrender every part of my life to You. I lay down my plans, my ambitions, and my desires, and I commit them into Your hands. I choose to live for You Lord, with all my heart, soul, mind, and strength. Help me to live a life that honors You in everything I do.

Renew my mind and transform my heart, that I may know and do Your will. Help me to grow in holiness and to reflect Your character in all my relationships. I offer my body, my time, my energy, and my resources to You, knowing that this is my true act of worship.

In Jesus' name, I pray. Amen.

H

PRAYERS FOR THE CHURCH AND MINISTRIES

36

PRAYER FOR THE CHURCH'S GROWTH
(ACTS 2:42-47)

The Church is God's instrument on earth to manifest His Kingdom, preach the gospel, and disciple nations. The growth of the Church is not just about numerical increase but also about spiritual maturity, unity, and impact in the world. Acts 2:42-47 gives us a clear picture of the early Church's commitment to prayer, teaching, fellowship, breaking of bread, and generosity. As a result, the Lord added to their number daily those who were being saved.

Why Pray for the Church's Growth?

1. *For Spiritual Maturity:* Growth in numbers must be accompanied by growth in faith, holiness, and knowledge of Christ (Ephesians 4:13-15).

2. *For Unity and Love:* A Church that is united in love will be a strong testimony to the world (John 17:21-23).

3. *For Evangelistic Zeal:* The mission of the Church is to reach the lost; prayer fuels passion for evangelism (Matthew 28:19-20).

4. *For the Power of the Holy Spirit:* True growth happens when the Church is filled with the Holy Spirit (Acts 1:8).

5. *For Protection Against Opposition:* The enemy seeks to hinder the growth of the Church through persecution, false doctrine, and division (Matthew 16:18).

Biblical Example of Church Growth

The early Church grew rapidly, not because of human efforts alone but because of their devotion to prayer and the power of the Holy Spirit. Acts 2:42-47 outlines key elements that contributed to their growth:

- *Steadfast in Doctrine:* They continued in the apostles' teaching.
- *Fellowship and Breaking of Bread:* They lived in unity and shared meals together.
- *Prayer:* They committed themselves to prayer continually.
- *Signs and Wonders:* God confirmed their ministry with miracles.
- *Generosity:* They shared their possessions to meet needs.
- *Daily Additions:* The Lord brought more people into the Church.

These principles remain relevant for today's Church. As we pray for growth, we must align ourselves with God's blueprint for a thriving Church.

How to Pray for the Church's Growth

1. *Pray for Sound Doctrine:* Ask God to raise teachers who will preach the pure Word of God without compromise (2 Timothy 4:2-3).

2. *Pray for a Revival of Prayer:* A praying Church is a growing Church. Pray for believers to commit to personal and corporate prayer (1 Thessalonians 5:17).

3. *Pray for Evangelistic Boldness:* Ask the Lord to anoint His people to share the gospel fearlessly (Acts 4:29-31).

4. *Pray for Unity and Love:* Pray that believers will walk in love, forgiveness, and unity (Colossians 3:13-14).

5. *Pray for Supernatural Manifestations:* Ask for signs, wonders, and miracles to accompany the preaching of the Word (Mark 16:20).

6. *Pray for Resources:* The Church needs financial and human resources to expand its work (Philippians 4:19).

7. *Pray for New Converts to be Discipled:* Growth is sustained when new believers are nurtured in faith (Matthew 28:20).

Sample Prayer for Church Growth

Heavenly Father, we thank You for the Church, Your body on earth. We pray for growth, both spiritually and numerically. Let Your Word be preached in truth and power. Fill the Church with a hunger for prayer and a passion for souls. Strengthen believers to walk in love and unity. Pour out Your Spirit, O Lord, and confirm Your Word with signs and wonders. Protect the Church from false teachings and divisions. Raise laborers for the harvest and provide all resources needed for expansion. Let the Church shine as a beacon of hope in a dark world. In Jesus' name, Amen.

The growth of the Church is God's will, it requires our partnership in prayer. By interceding for sound doctrine, revival, evangelistic passion, unity, and divine provision, we align with God's purpose to build His Church. As we pray and act in faith, we will witness the same power that grew the early Church manifest in our time. Let us commit to praying fervently for the advancement of God's Kingdom through His Church.

37

PRAYER FOR PASTORS AND LEADERS
(HEBREWS 13:17)

"Obey those who rule over you, and be submissive,
for they watch out for your souls, as those who must give account.
Let them do so with joy and not with grief,
for that would be unprofitable for you."

The Importance of Praying for Pastors and Leaders

Pastors and church leaders are called to shepherd God's people, guide them in truth, and stand in the gap spiritually. They carry a great responsibility, as they must give account for their ministry and the souls entrusted to them. The enemy continually seeks to discourage, deceive, and hinder their work. That is why prayer for pastors and leaders is vital.

Intercessory prayer strengthens them, refreshes their spirit, and shields them from attacks. A thriving pastor leads a thriving congregation. Our prayers help them stand firm, walk in wisdom, and fulfill God's will with joy.

Key Areas to Cover in Prayer

1. Spiritual Strength and Encouragement

- Pray for them to remain steadfast in faith, growing in their personal relationship with God.
- Ask the Lord to grant them fresh anointing, wisdom, and revelation for their ministry.
- Pray that they will not grow weary in well-doing (Galatians 6:9).

2. Protection and Divine Guidance

- Pray for their protection against spiritual attacks, temptations, and discouragement.
- Ask God to surround them with His angels and shield them from harm (Psalm 91:11-12).
- Pray for divine wisdom in decision-making, that they may lead with integrity and discernment.

3. Family and Personal Life

- Pray for their marriage and family to be strong, filled with love, peace, and unity.
- Ask God to bless their children and strengthen their household against any form of attack.
- Pray that they may have time to rest, refresh, and maintain balance between ministry and family.

4. Boldness in Preaching the Gospel

- Pray that they preach the Word of God with power and clarity (2 Timothy 4:2).
- Ask the Lord to remove every fear or hindrance that might cause them to compromise the truth.

- Pray for an outpouring of the Holy Spirit to confirm their message with signs and wonders (Mark 16:20).

5. Provision and Resources

- Pray for financial provision for their needs and the ministry work.
- Ask God to send faithful supporters who will uphold them through giving and encouragement.
- Pray for open doors for greater impact and for God's provision in every area of ministry.

A Sample Prayer for Pastors and Leaders

Heavenly Father,

We thank You for the pastors and leaders You have placed over us. We acknowledge that they are chosen vessels, called to shepherd Your people. Lord, we lift them up before You today, asking that You strengthen them with Your mighty power. Fill them with wisdom, knowledge, and understanding as they lead Your Church.

Father, protect them from every attack of the enemy. Guard their hearts against discouragement, deception, and distractions. Let them be refreshed daily in Your presence, drawing from the living waters of Your Spirit. Surround them with God-fearing and faithful people who will support and uplift them.

We pray for their families, that You may bless their homes with peace, love, and divine protection. May their children walk in Your ways, and may their marriages be strong and Christ-centered. Lord, supply all their needs according to Your riches in Glory, and open doors for greater impact in their ministry.

Grant them boldness to preach the gospel without compromise. Let them speak Your Word with power and conviction, and let signs and wonders follow to confirm the truth. May they lead with integrity, humility, and joy, fulfilling the call You have placed upon their lives.

In Jesus' name, we pray. Amen.

Encouragement for the Church

As members of the Body of Christ, we are called to support our pastors and leaders in every way possible. One of the greatest ways to do so is through consistent prayer. When we intercede for them, we contribute to the effectiveness of their ministry and the spiritual health of our Church. Let us be faithful in lifting them before the Lord, knowing that their victories are also ours.

"The effectual fervent prayer of a righteous man availeth much."
(James 5:16b)

38

PRAYER FOR REVIVAL AND AWAKENING
(2 CHRONICLES 7:14)

"If My people who are called by My name will humble themselves,
and pray and seek My Face, and turn from their wicked ways,
then I will hear from heaven, and will forgive their sin
and heal their land."

Understanding Revival and Awakening

Revival is the supernatural move of God that stirs the hearts of individuals, churches, and even entire nations to return to Him with fervor. It is a fresh outpouring of the Holy Spirit that ignites passion, holiness, and an earnest desire to seek God's face. Awakening, on the other hand, extends beyond the Church, bringing societal transformation as people come under conviction, turn from sin, and embrace the truth of the Gospel.

Throughout history, great revivals have marked spiritual reformation: such as the Welsh Revival, the Great Awakenings in America, and the Azusa Street Revival. These movements were birthed through fervent prayer, deep repentance, and a hunger for God's presence.

The Conditions for Revival

God's promise in 2 Chronicles 7:14 shows four essential conditions for revival:

1. *Humility:* Recognizing our dependence on God and surrendering pride.
2. *Prayer:* Seeking God's intervention with sincerity and persistence.
3. *Seeking His Face:* Developing an intimate relationship with Him rather than just seeking His blessings.
4. *Repentance:* Turning away from sinful ways and pursuing righteousness.

When these conditions are met, God promises to hear from Heaven, forgive sin, and bring healing to the land.

Praying for Revival and Awakening

Prayer is the key to unlocking divine revival. Below are different aspects of revival prayer:

1. Personal Revival

Revival begins in the heart of the believer. Pray for personal renewal and a rekindled fire for God:

- *Confess any known sins* and ask for cleansing (Psalm 51:10-12).
- *Pray for a fresh infilling of the Holy Spirit* (Ephesians 5:18).

- *Ask for a renewed hunger for God's Word and His presence* (Jeremiah 29:13).

2. Revival in the Church

The Church is the vessel through which God pours out revival. Pray for:

- A renewed passion for holiness and obedience among believers.
- Spiritual unity and an end to division (John 17:20-21).
- A return to fervent prayer and intercession (Acts 2:42-43).
- The restoration of spiritual gifts and the power of the Holy Spirit.

3. Revival in the Nation

National transformation happens when revival sweeps through societies. Pray for:

- National repentance and turning away from sin (Jonah 3:5-10).
- God to raise up righteous leaders who will honor Him (Proverbs 14:34).
- The Gospel to be preached with boldness and authority (Matthew 28:19-20).

Examples of Revival in the Bible

The Bible records several instances of revival, including:

- *The Revival under king Josiah (2 Kings 23:1-25):* The rediscovery of God's Word led to national repentance and covenant renewal.
- *The Revival at Pentecost (Acts 2):* The Holy Spirit's outpouring resulted in thousands being saved and the birth of the Church.

- *The Revival under Nehemiah and Ezra* (*Nehemiah 8-9*): A renewed commitment to God's law and mass repentance.

A Sample Prayer for Revival

Heavenly Father, we humble ourselves before You, acknowledging that we desperately need revival. Forgive us for our complacency and sin. Ignite within us a Holy fire and passion for Your presence. We pray for our churches, that they may return to You with fervent prayer and holiness. Let Your Spirit move mightily, bringing conviction, transformation, and an awakening across our land. Pour out Your mercy, heal our nation, and let the knowledge of Your Glory cover the earth as the waters cover the sea. In Jesus' name, Amen.

Revival and awakening are not just historical events but divine moves that can happen today. As we commit to persistent prayer, humility, and seeking God's Face, we position ourselves as vessels for His glory. May we remain faithful in praying for a mighty revival that will impact lives, churches, and nations for the Glory of God.

39

PRAYER FOR UNITY IN THE CHURCH
(JOHN 17:21)

"That they all may be one, as You, Father, are in Me,
and I in You; that they also may be one in Us,
that the world may believe that You sent Me."

The Heart of Jesus for Unity

Unity in the Church is the heartbeat of Jesus' final prayer before His crucifixion. He longed for His followers to be one, just as He and the Father are one. This unity is not just external agreement but a deep, spiritual oneness that reflects the divine nature of God. When the Church walks in unity, the world sees the love of Christ in action and is drawn to Him.

The Need for Unity in the Church

The enemy understands the power of unity, which is why he continually sows discord, division, and strife among believers. Differences in doctrine, cultural backgrounds, and personal opinions have often led to fragmentation in the Body of Christ. However, when the Church is united in love, purpose, and truth, it stands strong against the schemes of the enemy and advances God's Kingdom.

Benefits of Unity in the Church

Strength and Stability: A united Church is strong and resilient against the attacks of the enemy.

A Clear Testimony: The world sees Jesus through the love and unity of christians.

Power in Prayer: Corporate prayers in unity carry greater spiritual authority (Matthew 18:19-20).

Anointing and Blessings: God commands blessings where there is unity (Psalm 133:1-3).

How to Pray for Unity in the Church

Pray for Love Among Believers: Ask God to fill His people with His divine love, which brings them together in perfect unity (Colossians 3:14).

Pray Against the Spirit of Division: Rebuke the enemy's tactics of discord, gossip, and strife within the Church (1 Corinthians 1:10).

Pray for Humility and Servanthood: Unity thrives where there is humility and a willingness to serve one another (Philippians 2:3-4).

Pray for Doctrinal Soundness: Ask God to help believers remain grounded in His Word while embracing the diversity of gifts and callings in the Body (Ephesians 4:13-15).

Pray for a Shared Mission: Intercede for the Church to stay focused on the Great Commission and work together to spread the Gospel (Matthew 28:19-20).

A Model Prayer for Church Unity

Heavenly Father,

Thank You for the gift of the Church, the Body of Christ. You have called us to be one, and we come before You today, asking for unity among Your people. Remove every barrier that divides us: pride, offense, jealousy, and selfish ambition. Let Your love flow through us, knitting our hearts together in Christ.

Father, we rebuke every spirit of division and strife that seeks to weaken Your Church. We declare that we will walk in love, forgiveness, and humility. Help us to focus on what unites us rather than what separates us. May our unity be a testimony to the world that Jesus is Lord.

Fill our leaders with wisdom and discernment so they can shepherd the flock with grace. Give them the courage to promote unity and the boldness to stand firm in truth. Help each member of the Body to embrace their unique role while honoring and supporting one another.

Lord, empower us with a fresh outpouring of Your Spirit so that we may walk together in harmony, advancing Your Kingdom on earth. May our prayers, worship, and service reflect the unity that Jesus prayed for. We ask this in the mighty name of Jesus Christ. Amen.

Walking in Unity Daily

Unity is not something that happens overnight, it is cultivated daily. Here are some practical ways to maintain unity in the Church:

Practice Forgiveness: Let go of offenses quickly (Ephesians 4:32).

Encourage One Another: Build each other up in faith and love (1 Thessalonians 5:11).

Serve Together: Engage in Ministry with a team mindset (1 Corinthians 12:12-27).

Be Led by the Spirit: Allow the Holy Spirit to guide thoughts, actions, and words (Galatians 5:16-26).

Focus on the Mission: Keep Christ at the center of all activities and decisions (Colossians 3:17).

When we prioritize unity, we reflect the beauty of Christ's love to a divided world. The Church, walking in oneness, becomes an unstoppable force for God's Glory!

40

PRAYER FOR THE PERSECUTED CHURCH
(HEBREWS 13:3)

"Remember the prisoners as if chained with them;
those who are mistreated—
since you yourselves are in the body also."

Understanding the Persecution of the Church

The Body of Christ is one, and when one part suffers, the entire body feels it (1 Corinthians 12:26). Persecution has been a reality for believers since the early Church. Jesus Christ warned His disciples, saying, *"If they persecuted Me, they will also persecute you"* (John 15:20). Today, many of our brothers and sisters around the world face hostility, imprisonment, and other forms of persecutions for their faith in Christ.

Persecution takes many forms: verbal opposition, discrimination, physical harm, imprisonment, and more. However, the Bible encourages us to remember them in prayer, standing in the gap for their protection, strength, and endurance.

Why Should We Pray for the Persecuted Church?

It is a Biblical Command: Hebrews 13:3 instructs us to remember those in chains as though we were suffering with them.

They Need Strength to Endure: Persecuted believers often face extreme suffering and need divine strength to remain steadfast (2 Thessalonians 1:4-5).

To Encourage and Uplift Them: Our prayers can strengthen their faith, bringing them peace and comfort (Philippians 4:6-7).

To Advance the Gospel: Many persecuted believers continue to spread the Gospel despite opposition. Our prayers empower them to be bold witnesses (Acts 4:29).

God Can Intervene Miraculously: Just as Peter was delivered from prison through the prayers of the Church (Acts 12:5-11), God still works wonders for His people today.

How to Pray for the Persecuted Church

Pray for Protection: Ask God to shield them from harm and to frustrate the plans of the enemy (Psalm 91:1-4).

Pray for Strength and Endurance: That they may remain faithful under trial and receive supernatural courage (Isaiah 41:10, 2 Corinthians 12:9).

Pray for Provision: Many persecuted believers lack basic needs. Pray for God's provision of food, shelter, and medical care (Philippians 4:19).

Pray for Their Families: Many believers are separated from their loved ones due to persecution. Ask God to comfort their families and keep them safe (Psalm 68:5-6).

Pray for the Salvation of their persecutors: Jesus taught us to love our enemies and pray for those who persecute us (Matthew 5:44). Pray for their hearts to be transformed by the love of Christ.

A Sample Prayer for the Persecuted Church

Heavenly Father, we lift up our brothers and sisters who are facing persecution for their faith in You. Strengthen them with Your mighty power and let them not lose heart. Protect them from harm, provide for their needs, and fill them with Your peace that surpasses all understanding. Lord, let their testimonies shine as a beacon of hope, and may their persecutors come to know Your saving grace. We declare that no weapon formed against them shall prosper, and that Your Church will continue to grow despite opposition. In Jesus' name, Amen.

Encouraging Persecuted Believers

Aside from prayer, we can also support persecuted Christians through:

- *Raising awareness* in our churches and communities.
- *Supporting organizations* that provide aid and advocacy.
- *Writing letters* of encouragement to persecuted believers.
- *Being bold in our own faith,* standing firm against fear and intimidation.

As we pray for our brethren, we align ourselves with God's heart, demonstrating love, unity, and the power of intercession.

I

PRAYERS FOR FAMILY AND RELATIONSHIPS

41

PRAYER FOR MARRIAGE
(EPHESIANS 5:25)

"Husbands, love your wives,
just as Christ also loved the church
and gave Himself for her."

Marriage is a divine institution established by God to reflect His love, unity, and covenant relationship with His people. It is not just a social contract but a sacred bond requiring commitment, love, and mutual sacrifice between a man and a woman. Prayer for marriage is essential for couples to build a strong foundation, overcome challenges, and walk in unity according to God's purpose.

The Purpose of Marriage in God's Design

Marriage was instituted by God from the beginning (Genesis 2:24) as a union where a man and a woman become one flesh. This sacred covenant reflects Christ's love for the Church, where He sacrificed Himself to sanctify and nurture His bride. When couples understand this divine purpose, they can build their relationship on biblical principles rather than worldly expectations.

Prayer plays a vital role in marriage because it invites God's presence, wisdom, and guidance into the relationship. When couples pray together and for one another, they strengthen their spiritual bond and cultivate an atmosphere of love and peace.

Why Prayer for Marriage is Important

To Strengthen Love and Unity between husband and wife: Prayer keeps a marriage grounded in love, patience, and understanding.

For Protection from the Enemy: The enemy seeks to destroy marriages, but prayer creates a spiritual covering (John 10:10).

For Wisdom and Guidance: Couples need divine wisdom to navigate the challenges of life together (James 1:5).

To Build a Godly Legacy: A Christ-centered marriage impacts children and future generations positively (Proverbs 22:6).

Prayers for a Strong and Godly Marriage

1. Prayer for Love and Understanding

Heavenly Father, we thank You for the gift of marriage. Teach us to love one another as Christ loves the Church. Fill our hearts with patience, kindness, and understanding. Help us to walk in unity and cherish each other daily. Let our love be rooted in You so that we may reflect Your divine purpose. In Jesus' name, Amen.

2. Prayer for Protection Over Marriage

Lord, we ask for Your divine protection over our marriage. Guard our hearts against the attacks of the enemy, and help us to remain faithful and committed to each other. Shield our home from division, misunderstanding, and external influences that seek to destroy our union. We declare that our marriage will thrive in Your presence, in Jesus' name, Amen.

3. Prayer for Wisdom and Communication

Father, grant us wisdom to handle every situation in our marriage with grace. Help us to communicate effectively, listen with open hearts, and resolve conflicts with humility. Teach us to speak words that build each other up and not tear down. May our conversations be filled with love and encouragement, in Jesus' name, Amen.

4. Prayer for Fruitfulness in Marriage

Lord, we pray that our marriage will bear fruit in every area of life. Bless us with joy, peace, and prosperity. Grant us the blessing of children and help us raise them in Your ways. Let our home be a testimony of Your faithfulness and grace, in Jesus' name, Amen.

5. Prayer for a Christ-Centered Marriage

Lord Jesus Christ, be the foundation of our marriage. Help us to always seek You first in all that we do. May our relationship glorify You and be a light to others. Strengthen our faith, deepen our love, and help us to walk in obedience to Your Word. We surrender our marriage to You, trusting that You will lead and sustain us, in Jesus' name, Amen.

Marriage is a beautiful gift from God, meant to reflect His love, commitment, and unity between a man and a woman. Through consistent prayer, couples can overcome challenges, grow in love, and fulfill their God-given purpose together. As we pray for our marriages, let us trust in God's grace to strengthen and sustain our union, making it a powerful testimony of His faithfulness.

42

PRAYER FOR CHILDREN
(PROVERBS 22:6)

*"Train up a child in the way he should go:
and when he is old, he will not depart from it."*

"Children are a heritage from the Lord" (Psalm 127:3). As parents, guardians, or intercessors, we are called to lift them up in prayer. The world today is filled with distractions and challenges that can draw children away from God's purpose for their lives. Therefore, praying for children is not only an act of love but a spiritual responsibility.

Why Pray for Children?

For Their Spiritual Growth: That they may know God early and walk in His ways (Ecclesiastes 12:1).

For Protection: That God may keep them safe from harm and evil influences (Psalm 91:11-12).

For Wisdom and Understanding: That they may grow in wisdom and favor before God and man (Luke 2:52).

For Righteous Friendships: That they will be surrounded by Godly influences (Proverbs 13:20).

For Their Purpose and Destiny: That they will fulfill God's plan for their lives (Jeremiah 29:11).

How to Pray for Children

1. Prayer for Salvation and Spiritual Growth

Heavenly Father, I commit (children's names) into Your hands. Let Your Holy Spirit draw them close to You from a young age. Open their hearts to receive Your truth and walk in Your ways all the days of their lives. May they grow in faith, love, and obedience to You. In Jesus' name, Amen.

2. Prayer for Protection and Safety

Lord, I cover (children's names) with the precious blood of Jesus. No weapon formed against them shall prosper. Guard their going out and coming in. Assign Your angels to watch over them and shield them from harm and bad influences. I rebuke every plan of the enemy against their lives. In Jesus' mighty name, Amen.

3. Prayer for Wisdom and Academic Excellence

Father, grant (children's names) wisdom, knowledge, and understanding. Let them excel in their studies and grow in intelligence and discipline. Give them the love for learning and the ability to grasp and retain knowledge. May they be light in their school and examples of Godliness. In Jesus' name, Amen.

4. Prayer for Friendships and Godly Influence

Lord, surround (children's names) with the right friends who will encourage them in righteousness. Remove every negative influence and place them in relationships that will help them grow in faith and wisdom. Let them be a light and not be led astray by worldly temptations. In Jesus' name, Amen.

5. Prayer for Their Future and Destiny

Father, I commit (children's names) into Your hands. You created them with a purpose. Let them discover and walk in Your divine plan. May they become leaders and Kingdom builders, influencing their generation for Christ. I cancel every plan of the enemy that seeks to derail them from their destiny. Let Your will alone be done in their lives. In Jesus' name, Amen.

Encouragement for Parents

Raising children in the fear of the Lord requires prayer, patience, and faith. Trust that God hears and answers your prayers for your children. Remember, the seeds of faith sown in their hearts will not be in vain. Keep declaring God's promises over their lives and be an example of His love and grace.

Children are precious in the sight of God. Through consistent prayer, we can shape their lives according to God's purpose. Proverbs 22:6 assures us that when we train them in the right way, they will not depart from it. Let us continue to stand in the gap for them, knowing that our prayers will yield great results in their lives.

43

PRAYER FOR RESTORATION OF RELATIONSHIPS
(2 CORINTHIANS 5:18)

"Now all things are of God,
who has reconciled us to Himself through Jesus Christ,
and has given us the ministry of reconciliation."

Understanding the Ministry of Reconciliation

God is a God of restoration. One of the clearest demonstrations of His love is seen in how He reconciled the world to Himself through Jesus Christ. In 2 Corinthians 5:18, we see that not only has He restored our relationship with Him, but He has also entrusted us with the ministry of reconciliation. This ministry is not only spiritual, between God and man, but also practical, between humans.

Broken relationships whether in families, churches, marriages, friendships, or among colleagues are an opportunity for believers to bring God's healing power into emotional and relational pain.

The devil delights in division. He comes to steal, kill, and destroy (John 10:10), and one of his chief weapons is relational strife. He sows offense, bitterness, and misunderstanding, turning hearts away from one another. But God calls us to be peacemakers. Restoration is not about ignoring pain or pretending wounds don't exist; it's about allowing the Holy Spirit to work in us to bring genuine healing, forgiveness, and renewed connection.

Why Relationships Matter to God

From the beginning, God created us for relationships. When He saw Adam alone in the garden, He said, *"It is not good for man to be alone."* God Himself exists in relationship Father, Son, and Holy Spirit. Our relationships reflect the heart of God and are part of His Kingdom purpose. Jesus summarized the law and the prophets into two commandments: *love God and love your neighbor* (Matthew 22:37-40). This shows how deeply God values connection.

When relationships are broken, something of God's intention for our lives is hindered. That's why Jesus tells us in Matthew 5:23-24 that if we are offering our gift at the altar and remember our brother has something against us, we should first go and be reconciled. This means God places a high priority on unity and restored fellowship.

Prayer is a tool for relationship restoration. It humbles us, aligns us with God's heart, and releases spiritual authority to break the barriers of pride, pain, and miscommunication. Through prayer, we invite the Prince of Peace into our situations.

A Prayer Guide for Relationship Restoration

Heavenly Father,

I thank You for reconciling me to Yourself through Jesus Christ. You have poured out mercy, forgiveness, and unconditional love toward me. Now, Lord, I ask You to help me walk in that same spirit of reconciliation.

I lift up every broken relationship in my life; whether with family, friends, or fellow believers. I ask for Your healing power to move into those areas of hurt, offense, betrayal, and misunderstanding.

I forgive those who have wounded me, and I ask You to forgive me where I have caused pain. Remove every root of bitterness, pride, and anger. Soften our hearts and open our eyes to each other's value and perspective.

I bind every demonic influence working to keep us apart and declare that love, peace, and restoration will reign.

Teach me how to walk in humility and wisdom. Show me when to speak, when to listen, and when to be silent. Use me as Your vessel of reconciliation, first in my family, then in my church, and even in my community.

Let our restored relationships be a testimony of Your power. May Your love unite us together perfectly .

In Jesus' name, Amen.

44

PRAYER FOR GENERATIONAL BLESSINGS
(PSALM 112:2)

Introduction to Generational Blessings

Generational blessings are a profound expression of God's covenantal faithfulness passed down from one generation to another. Psalm 112:2 declares, *"His descendants will be mighty on earth; the generation of the upright will be blessed."* This promise is not just for the individual but extends to their children and grandchildren, reflecting the depth of God's love and His desire to bless families for generations.

In this prayer, we will focus on invoking God's blessings upon our descendants, asking for His favor, protection, and prosperity to follow them throughout their lives. It is an acknowledgment that our lives are intertwined with the future of our children, grandchildren, great-grandchildren, and many future generations. The prayer also serves as a petition for God to raise up leaders, righteous men and women, and individuals who will honor Him, fulfill their divine purpose, and continue the legacy of faith.

Understanding Psalm 112:2

Psalm 112 is a beautiful Psalm that speaks about the blessings and benefits of living a righteous life. Verse 2 highlights the generational impact of upright living, saying, *"His descendants will be mighty on earth."* This powerful promise assures us that living according to God's will not only impacts our immediate lives but will also shape the destiny of future generations.

The promise that *"the generation of the upright will be blessed"* shows God's desire to establish a legacy of righteousness, wisdom, and spiritual prosperity. A generational blessing doesn't only refer to material wealth but also to spiritual growth, peace, health, and the favor of God resting upon successive generations.

The Role of Righteousness in Generational Blessings

In this passage, we see that the key to experiencing generational blessings is righteousness. Psalm 112:1 begins with an exhortation to the righteous, saying, *"Praise the Lord! Blessed is the man who fears the Lord, who delights greatly in His commandments"* Righteous living is the foundation upon which blessings are built. When we walk uprightly before God, we align ourselves with His will and open the door to His favor, not only for us but for those who come after us.

As parents and leaders, it is essential to model righteous behavior for our children and those in our influence. The way we live today can impact not only our lives but the trajectory of our families for generations to come.

Praying for Generational Blessings

Let us now turn to prayer. Begin by recognizing God as the Source of all blessings and honor Him for His faithfulness to our families. Acknowledge your desire to see your family walk in His favor and righteousness, praying that His blessings would overflow onto your descendants.

Prayer for Generational Blessings:

Father God,

I come before You today in awe of Your greatness and Your love that extends from generation to generation. Thank You for Your covenant promise that You will bless the descendants of the righteous.

Lord, I lift up my family before You, asking that Your blessings be poured out upon my children, my grandchildren, my great-grandchildren and all future generations. May they be mighty on the earth, walking in Your ways, guided by Your wisdom, and protected by Your mighty hand.

I pray that my descendants will be known for their righteousness, their love for You, and their commitment to Your Word. May they be a generation that honors You with their lives and brings glory to Your name.

I ask that You would raise up leaders among them; those who will lead with integrity, who will be bold in their faith, and who will stand for justice and truth. May they fulfill the purposes You have set before them and walk in the fullness of Your blessing.

Father, I pray for spiritual prosperity for my family. May they experience peace, joy, and abundant life, all through Your grace. Bless their relationships, their health, their work, and their finances. May Your favor rest upon them in every area of their lives.

I thank You for the inheritance of blessings You are preparing for my family. I trust in Your promises, and I declare that my household is blessed in the name of Jesus. Amen.

Meditating on Generational Blessings

As you pray for generational blessings, take time to meditate on the significance of your prayers. Think about the impact your life can have on your descendants. How can you model faithfulness and righteousness for your children, your grandchildren, your great-grandchildren and all future generations?

Generational blessings come not only through prayer but also through the actions and choices we make today. Choose to live in a way that honors God, knowing that your decisions will affect not only your present but also the future of your loved ones.

Scriptural Affirmations for Generational Blessings

1. *"The righteous man walks in his integrity; His children are blessed after him."* Proverbs 20:7

2. *"And all your children shall be taught by the Lord, and great shall be the peace of your children."* Isaiah 54:13

3. *"Blessed is the man who fears the Lord, who greatly delights in His commandments. His descendants will be mighty on earth."* Psalm 112:1-2

4. *"I have been young, and now am old; Yet I have not seen the righteous forsaken, Nor his descendants begging bread."* Psalm 37:25

5. *"The mercy of the Lord is from everlasting to everlasting on those who fear Him, And His righteousness to children's children."* Psalm 103:17

As you reflect on these verses, speak them over your family. Declare that God's blessings will be upon your household for generations to come. Trust that He is faithful to fulfill His promises.

Living Out Generational Blessings

Living out generational blessings involves actively engaging in God's plan for your family. It means teaching your children the Word of God, leading them in prayer, and living as a Godly example. It also involves praying for future generations and believing that God will honor the prayers you offer today.

In addition, it's essential to live in such a way that your descendants will inherit not only material blessings but also spiritual inheritance; the knowledge of God's Word, a passion for prayer, and a heart to serve Him.

Prayer for generational blessings is an act of faith and obedience. When we pray for the generations that come after us, we partner with God in His eternal plan. Psalm 112:2 reminds us that God desires to bless our families, not just for a season but for eternity.

May this prayer be a starting point for you as you seek God's blessings for your family. Let the promises in Scripture encourage you to live righteously and to deliver a legacy of faith that will last for generations.

45

PRAYER FOR PROTECTION OVER FAMILY
(PSALM 91:10-11)

"No evil shall befall you,
nor shall any plague come near your dwelling;
for He shall give His angels charge over you,
to keep you in all your ways."

The Need for Divine Protection

In a world filled with uncertainties, dangers, and spiritual battles, one of the greatest prayers we can offer is for the protection over our family. God, in His infinite love and wisdom, has provided us with promises of safety and security through His Word. Psalm 91 is a powerful declaration of divine protection, assuring believers that no harm will come near their dwelling because of the Lord's covering.

It is no coincidence to my discerning heart that the emergency number 911 in America echoes the powerful promise found in Psalm 91:1 *"He who dwells in the secret place of the Most High shall abide under the Shadow of the Almighty."* While the number 911 was chosen for practical reasons, many believers see a divine parallel: in times of crisis, just as people call 911 for urgent help, we can turn to Psalm 91:1 and find refuge, protection, and immediate spiritual intervention from the Most High God.

The enemy seeks to attack families, bringing division, sickness, and fear. However, as believers, we have the authority to stand in prayer, declaring God's promises over our households. The power of intercession can set a hedge of divine protection around our loved ones, ensuring that no evil befalls them.

The Role of Angels in Protection

Psalm 91:11 specifically mentions that God commands His angels to guard us in all our ways. Angels are ministering spirits sent by God to protect and guide His people (Hebrews 1:14). Throughout the Bible, we see instances where angels intervened in the lives of God's people, shielding them from harm.

- In Exodus 23:20, God assured Israel that He would send an angel ahead of them to guard them on their journey.
- In Daniel 6:22, an angel shut the mouths of the lions, protecting Daniel from harm.
- In Acts 12:7, an angel freed Peter from prison, leading him to safety.

These accounts demonstrate that divine protection is real, and God still assigns His angels to watch over families who seek His covering.

Declaring God's Protection Over Your Family

Prayer is the key to activating the promises of God. When we pray for protection, we invite the presence of The Almighty to cover our family. Here is a prayer based on Psalm 91:10-11

Prayer for Family Protection

Heavenly Father, I thank You for the promise of protection You have given us in Your Word. According to Psalm 91, I declare that no evil shall befall my family, and no plague shall come near our home. I ask that You give Your angels charge over us, to guard us in all our ways. Let Your presence be a shield around us, and may Your peace reign in our hearts. Cover my spouse, my children, and every member of my household under the shadow of Your wings. Keep us safe from harm, sickness, accidents, and any form of attack from the enemy. In Jesus' mighty name, Amen.

Living Under God's Protection

While praying for protection is essential, we must also live in obedience to God's Word. Psalm 91 begins with the condition, *"He who dwells in the secret place of the Most High shall abide under the shadow of the Almighty"* (Psalm 91:1). This means that those who remain close to God in prayer, worship, and righteous living will experience His divine covering.

Here are some practical ways to ensure God's protection over your family:

Commit Your Family to God Daily: Pray over your spouse, children, and home each morning and evening, declaring God's promises.

Speak God's Word Over Your Home: Read and confess protective scriptures like Psalm 91, Isaiah 54:17 *"No weapon formed against you shall prosper"*, and Proverbs 18:10 *"The name of the Lord is a strong tower; the righteous run to it and are safe"*.

Anoint Your Home: Just as the Israelites applied the blood of the lamb over their doorposts (Exodus 12:7), you can anoint your home with oil as a sign of dedication to God.

Live in Holiness: Avoid anything that invites darkness into your home, such as ungodly influences, fear, or strife.

Trust in God's Sovereignty: Always trust that God is your refuge and fortress (Psalm 91:2).

The power of prayer for family protection cannot be underestimated. As believers, we must stand firm on God's promises and intercede for our loved ones. Psalm 91 assures us that no evil will come near us when we abide under God's divine covering. Let us continue to pray, trust, and declare His faithfulness, knowing that He is our refuge, our stronghold, and the ultimate protector of our families.

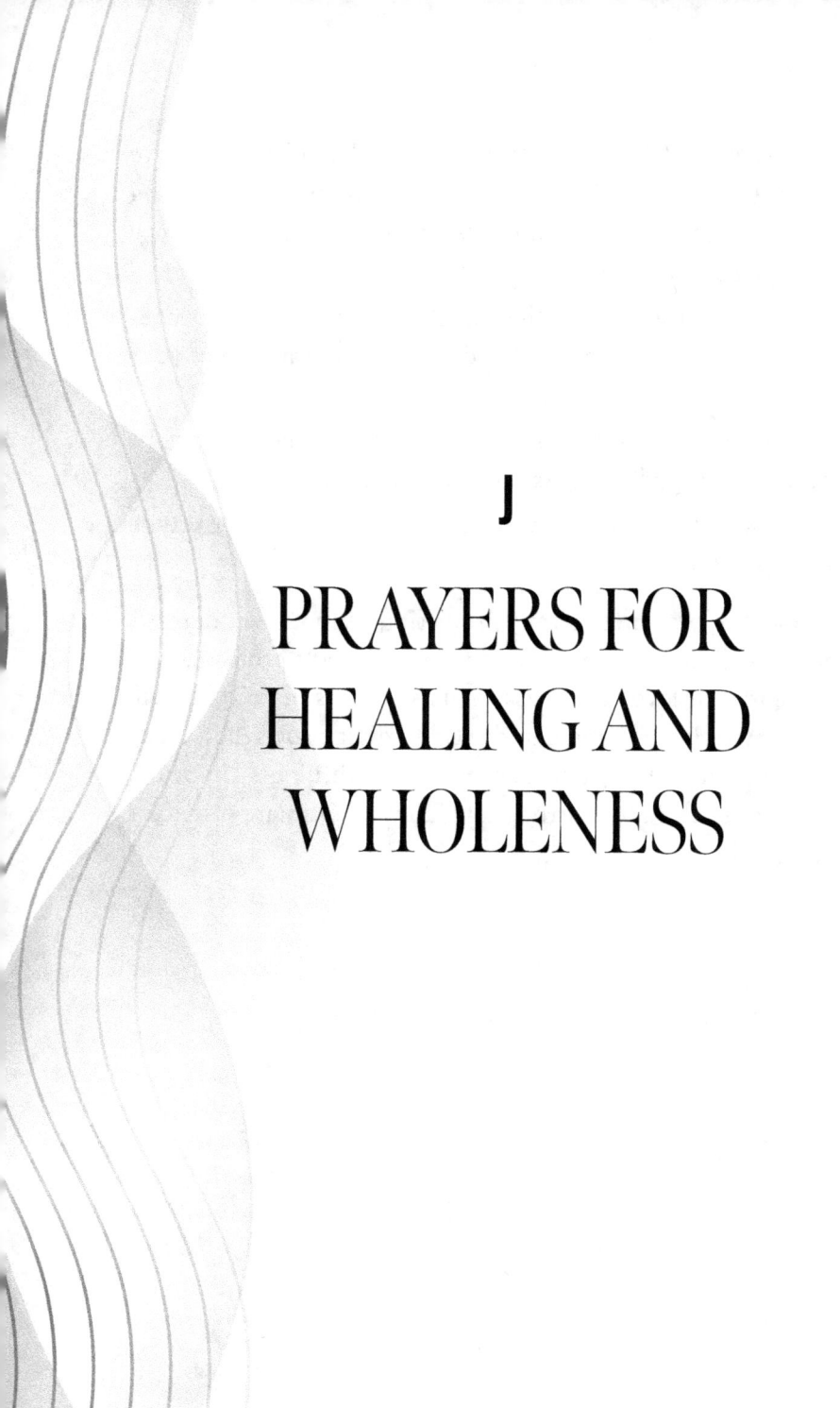

J

PRAYERS FOR HEALING AND WHOLENESS

46

PRAYER FOR PHYSICAL HEALING
(JAMES 5:14-15)

*"Is anyone among you sick? Let him call for the elders of the church,
and let them pray over him, anointing him with oil in the name of the Lord.
15And the prayer of faith will save the sick, and the Lord will raise him up.
And if he has committed sins, he will be forgiven."*

Understanding the Prayer for Physical Healing

Physical healing has always been part of God's covenant with His people. From the Old Testament to the New Testament, God reveals Himself as Jehovah Rapha, the Lord who heals (Exodus 15:26). Believers are encouraged to turn to God in prayer, seeking His divine intervention for healing.

James 5:14-15 provides a biblical model for praying for healing. It instructs the sick to call for the elders, who will anoint them with oil and pray in faith. This passage shows key principles of healing prayer: the role of faith, the importance of communal prayer, and the connection between spiritual and physical well-being.

Biblical Examples of Physical Healing

The Bible is full of accounts where God miraculously healed individuals who called upon Him:

- *The Woman with the Issue of Blood* (Mark 5:25-34) After suffering for twelve years, she touched the hem of Jesus' garment in faith and was healed instantly.
- *The Healing of the Lame Man* (Acts 3:1-10) Through the prayer and faith of Peter and John, a man who was lame from birth received strength in his legs and began to walk.

These examples show that healing comes through faith, persistence in prayer, and the power of God's Word.

Keys to Effective Prayer for Healing

Faith in God's Power: Faith is essential for healing. James 5:15 states that *"the prayer offered in faith"* brings healing. Jesus often told those He healed, *"Your faith has made you whole."*

Anointing with Oil: The Bible encourages the use of anointing oil as a symbol of the Holy Spirit's power and God's healing presence (Mark 6:13).

Confession and Repentance: Sometimes, sickness may be linked to sin. James 5:16 advises believers to confess their sins and pray for one another to receive healing.

Praying in Agreement: Matthew 18:19 says that if two believers agree in prayer as touching anything, God will answer. Corporate prayer strengthens faith and invites God's power.

Declaring God's Word: Speaking healing scriptures over your body builds faith and aligns your mind with God's promises. Verses like Isaiah 53:5 *"By His wounds, we are healed"* affirm God's will for health.

Sample Prayer for Physical Healing

Heavenly Father,

I come before You today, standing on Your promise that You are the God who heals. I lift up my body (or the person I am praying for), and I ask for Your healing touch. Your Word says that the prayer of faith will heal the sick, and I trust in Your power. Lord, if there is any sin that needs to be confessed, reveal it so that nothing hinders this prayer. I rebuke sickness and disease in Jesus' name and declare health, strength, and restoration over my body. Let Your healing virtue flow through me, restoring every organ and cell. I receive my healing by faith, in Jesus' mighty name. Amen.

Healing prayer is a powerful way to invite God's intervention into our lives. Whether through personal prayer, the anointing of oil, or the agreement of believers, God's healing power is available to those who seek Him in faith. As you continue to pray for healing, stand firm on God's promises, knowing that He is faithful to answer.

47

PRAYER FOR EMOTIONAL HEALING
(PSALM 34:18)

"The Lord is near to those who have a broken heart,
And saves such as have a contrite spirit."

Understanding Emotional Healing Through Prayer

The human heart, though resilient, sometimes needs divine intervention for full restoration. Prayer is a powerful means through which God heals emotional wounds and restores inner peace.

The Bible assures us that God is near to the brokenhearted. When we feel overwhelmed by sorrow, fear, or anxiety, we can turn to Him in prayer. His presence brings comfort, and His love provides healing that surpasses human understanding. The Holy Spirit, our Comforter, helps us process our emotions, guiding us toward peace and joy.

Biblical Examples of Emotional Healing

Hannah's Prayer (1 Samuel 1:10-20) Hannah was deeply distressed because of barrenness and societal pressure. She poured out her soul before the Lord, and God granted her peace and answered her prayer.

David's Lament and Restoration (Psalm 42, Psalm 51) David expressed his sorrow and struggles through heartfelt prayers, and God restored his joy.

How to Pray for Emotional Healing

Acknowledge Your Pain: Be honest with God about your feelings. Pour out your heart as Hannah did.

Declare God's Promises: Meditate on scriptures like Psalm 34:18, Isaiah 61:1, and Matthew 11:28-30.

Forgive and Release: Emotional healing often requires forgiving those who have hurt you (Ephesians 4:32).

Invite the Holy Spirit: Allow the Holy Spirit to minister to your heart, bringing comfort and renewal.

Cultivate a Lifestyle of Worship: Worship shifts focus from pain to God's goodness, bringing supernatural peace.

A Sample Prayer for Emotional Healing

Heavenly Father,

Your Word says that You are close to the brokenhearted and that You heal those who are crushed in spirit. Lord, I lay my wounds before You, asking for Your healing touch upon my emotions.

Help me to release bitterness, unforgiveness, and resentment. Fill me with Your peace and restore my joy. Let Your Holy Spirit comfort me, renewing my heart and mind. I trust in Your love and power to bring total restoration. Thank You for hearing my prayer. In Jesus' name, Amen.

Walking in Emotional Wholeness

After praying for healing, take practical steps to maintain emotional health:

- Surround yourself with supportive believers.
- Engage in regular Bible study and prayer.
- Speak positive affirmations based on God's Word.
- Seek counseling if needed, as God also works through wise counsel.

God is faithful to heal and restore. As you continue in prayer and faith, you will experience His peace that surpasses understanding (Philippians 4:7).

48

PRAYER FOR HEALING OF THE LAND
(2 CHRONICLES 7:14)

"If My people who are called by My name will humble themselves,
and pray and seek My face, and turn from their wicked ways,
then I will hear from heaven, and will forgive their sin and heal their land."

Understanding the Need for Healing of the Land

The land we live in can suffer because of sin, injustice, idolatry, and disobedience to God. When nations turn away from God, the land itself bears the consequences; droughts, natural disasters, economic downturns, and moral decay. However, God has given His people a clear prescription for healing: humility, prayer, seeking His face, and repentance.

Healing of the land is not just about physical restoration but also spiritual revival. God desires to bring righteousness, peace, and prosperity to nations that honor Him. Our prayers can invite divine intervention to restore and transform our communities.

The Components of a Prayer for Healing of the Land

Humility Before God

True healing starts with humility. As believers, we must acknowledge that we need God's intervention. Pride and self-reliance prevent healing, but humility opens the door to God's grace (James 4:6).

Repentance and Turning from Sin

Confession of national and personal sins is essential. We must stand in the gap for our land, repenting on behalf of our nation, just as Daniel did (Daniel 9:3-19).

Seeking God's Face

Seeking God goes beyond casual prayers; it requires a passionate pursuit of His presence through fasting, worship, and obedience. When we seek Him wholeheartedly, He responds (Jeremiah 29:13).

God's Promise to Hear and Heal

When we follow these steps, God promises to hear from heaven, forgive our sins, and heal the land. His faithfulness guarantees that our prayers, when aligned with His will, will bring transformation.

A Sample Prayer for Healing of the Land

Heavenly Father,

We come before You with humble hearts, acknowledging that You alone are the Sovereign Lord over our land. We confess that as a nation, we have sinned against You in many ways; through injustice, idolatry, immorality, and neglect of Your ways. Lord, have mercy on us.

We repent on behalf of our people, leaders, and generations past. Forgive us for turning away from Your truth. Cleanse our land from every form of unrighteousness. Remove corruption, oppression, and division from among us.

Lord, we seek Your face today. Pour out Your Spirit upon our nation. Revive Your Church so that we may be a light in the darkness. Let righteousness and justice prevail in our society.

Father, heal our land. Restore what has been destroyed. Bring physical and spiritual renewal. Let the land yield its increase, and let peace reign within our borders.

We declare that Jesus Christ is Lord over this land! We give You all the glory, honor, and praise. In Jesus' mighty name, we pray. Amen.

Prayer for healing of the land is a crucial responsibility of believers. When we intercede with sincerity and faith, God hears and moves on our behalf. As we commit to living righteously and seeking God continually, we will witness His healing power transforming our families, communities, and nations.

49

PRAYER FOR INNER PEACE
(PHILIPPIANS 4:7)

"And the peace of God, which surpasses all understanding,
will guard your hearts and minds through Christ Jesus."

The Need for Inner Peace

God promises His children a peace that goes beyond human comprehension; a divine peace that anchors the soul in the midst of storms. This peace is not found in worldly solutions but is a gift from God through Jesus Christ.

Understanding God's Peace

The peace of God is different from the temporary relief that the world offers. It is not only the absence of trouble but the presence of God's assurance, in every circumstances. Jesus Christ said in John 14:27, *"Peace I leave with you; My peace I give to you; not as the world gives do I give to you. Let not your heart be troubled, neither let it be afraid."* This shows that divine peace is independent of external situations; it is an inner tranquility that only God can provide.

Apostle Paul, in Philippians 4:6-7, instructs believers to present their worries to God in prayer, with thanksgiving. As a result, the peace of God, which is beyond human reasoning, will guard their hearts and minds. This guarding is like a divine shield, protecting one's thoughts and emotions from the attacks of fear, worry, and doubt.

How to Pray for Inner Peace

Acknowledge God as Your Source of Peace

Begin your prayer by recognizing that true peace comes from God alone. Thank Him for His faithfulness and for the promise of peace in His Word.

Prayer Example:

Heavenly Father, I acknowledging that You alone are my Peace. I thank You for Your promise in Philippians 4:7 that Your peace, which surpasses all understanding, will guard my heart and mind through Christ Jesus. I trust in You, Lord.

Cast Your Burdens on the Lord

Surrender your worries, fears, and anxieties to God. Speak to Him about what is troubling you and lay it all at His feet.

Prayer Example:

Lord, You see the burdens I carry; the anxieties, the uncertainties, and the fears that try to overwhelm me. I lay them before You, knowing that You care for me. I release every worry into Your hands and trust You to work all things for my good.

Ask for the Peace of Christ to Fill Your Heart

Invite the Holy Spirit to fill you with divine peace that surpasses all understanding. Ask for His presence to calm your heart and mind.

Prayer Example:

Holy Spirit, I invite You to fill my heart with Your peace. Let the peace of Christ rule in my heart and silence every fear. I reject the spirit of anxiety and embrace Your perfect peace that guards my mind.

Meditate on God's Promises

Declare Scriptures that reinforce God's peace in your life. Meditate on them and allow them to renew your mind.

Key Scriptures:

Isaiah 26:3 *"You will keep him in perfect peace, whose mind is stayed on You, because he trusts in You."*

2 Thessalonians 3:16 *"Now may the Lord of peace Himself give you peace always in every way. The Lord be with you all."*

Living in the Peace of God

Inner peace is not a one-time experience but a daily walk with God. Here are some ways to maintain this peace:

- *Spend Time in Prayer Daily:* Consistently bring your cares before God and allow Him to renew your peace each day.
- *Trust in God's Plan:* Even when things seem uncertain, trust that God is in control and that His plans for you are good (Jeremiah 29:11).

- *Guard Your Heart and Mind:* Be mindful of what you expose yourself to whether through media, conversations, or thoughts. Focus on things that build faith and bring peace (Philippians 4:8).
- *Stay in Fellowship with Believers:* Surround yourself with people who encourage your faith and remind you of God's promises.

The peace of God is a powerful gift that every believer can access through prayer and faith. No matter what challenges arise, His peace can guard your heart and mind, keeping you steady and secure. As you continue to seek Him, trust in His promises, and release your burdens in prayer, you will walk in the fullness of His divine peace, experiencing His rest always.

Prayer Declaration

Lord, I choose to abide in Your peace today. I reject fear, anxiety, and worry, and I embrace the peace that You freely give. Thank You, Lord, for guarding my heart and mind with Your perfect peace. In Jesus' name, Amen.

50

PRAYER FOR
BREAKING CURSES
(GALATIANS 3:13)

A curse is a spiritual limitation or hardship imposed upon a person, family, or generation due to sin, disobedience, or demonic influence. Many people unknowingly live under curses that hinder progress, health, and spiritual growth. The good news is that Jesus Christ has redeemed us from the curse of the law by becoming a curse for us (Galatians 3:13). Through faith and prayer, we can break free from every curse and walk in the blessings of God.

Understanding Curses

Curses can originate from various sources:

Generational Curses: Passed down through family lines due to ancestral sins (Exodus 20:5).

Self-Imposed Curses: Spoken over oneself in moments of despair (Proverbs 18:21).

Witchcraft and Occultic Curses: Pronounced by evil forces or individuals engaging in dark practices (Numbers 22:6).

Disobedience to God: Rebellion against God's commands (Deuteronomy 28:15-19).

Curses from Others: Words spoken in anger or envy can have spiritual effects if not countered, so we need to counter every evil pronouncement (James 3:8-10).

Biblical Basis for Breaking Curses

Galatians 3:13-14 *"Christ has redeemed us from the curse of the law, having become a curse for us (for it is written, "Cursed is everyone who hangs on a tree"), ¹⁴ that the blessing of Abraham might come upon the Gentiles in Christ Jesus, that we might receive the promise of the Spirit through faith."*

Colossians 2:14-15 *"Blotting out the handwriting of ordinances that was against us, which was contrary to us, and took it out of the way, nailing it to his cross; ¹⁵ And having spoiled principalities and powers, he made a shew of them openly, triumphing over them in it."*

Proverbs 26:2 *"As the bird by wandering, as the swallow by flying, so the curse causeless shall not come."*

Isaiah 54:17 *"No weapon that is formed against thee shall prosper; and every tongue that shall rise against thee in judgment thou shalt condemn. This is the heritage of the servants of the Lord, and their righteousness is of me, saith the Lord."*

2 Corinthians 5:17 *"Therefore if any man be in Christ, he is a new creature: old things are passed away; behold, all things are become new."*

Steps to Breaking Curses Through Prayer

1. *Repentance and Confession:* Acknowledge any known sins, renounce them, and seek God's forgiveness (1 John 1:9).

2. *Renounce the Curse:* Verbally reject and break agreement with any curse operating in your life.

3. *Declare Christ's Redemption:* Proclaim Galatians 3:13 and other scriptures to affirm your freedom.

4. *Cancel Negative Words:* Reject any negative words spoken over you and declare God's promises (Matthew 12:37).

5. *Pray with Authority:* Use the name of Jesus and the power of His blood to break all curses (Luke 10:19).

6. *Replace Curses with Blessings*: Speak God's blessings over your life, family, and future (Deuteronomy 28:1-14).

Prayer for Breaking Curses

Heavenly Father, I come before You in the name of Jesus Christ. I repent of any sins in my life and in my family line that have given the enemy a foothold. I renounce and break every generational curse, self-imposed curse, and spoken curse over my life. According to Galatians 3:13, I declare that Christ has redeemed me from the curse of the law. I cancel every demonic assignment against me and command all evil influences to leave in Jesus' name. No weapon formed against me shall prosper, and every tongue that rises against me in judgment, I condemn. I walk in the freedom, blessing, and abundance of Christ. Amen.

Living in the Freedom of Christ

After breaking curses, it is important to fill your life with God's Word, live in obedience, and maintain a lifestyle of prayer. Surround yourself with Godly people, speak blessings over your life daily, and remain steadfast in faith, knowing that Jesus Christ has set you free. Amen!

K

PRAYERS FOR NATIONS AND GOVERNMENTS

51

PRAYER FOR THE NATION
(1 TIMOTHY 2:2)

"For kings, and for all that are in authority;
that we may lead a quiet and peaceable life
in all Godliness and honesty."

The Biblical Mandate for Praying for the Nation

God commands His people to pray for their nations, particularly for those in authority. Paul's exhortation to Timothy shows that intercession for leaders leads to a peaceful and Godly society. A nation flourishes when its leaders act with wisdom, justice, and righteousness. As believers, we have a duty to stand in the gap, lifting our nation before the throne of grace.

Why Pray for the Nation?

1. *For Peace and Stability:* When leaders make wise decisions, the nation enjoys stability and security. (Proverbs 29:2)
2. *For Righteous Governance:* Godly leaders promote justice, while ungodly leadership leads to corruption and oppression. (Proverbs 14:34)

3. *For Spiritual Awakening:* National revival begins when believers intercede for their land. (2 Chronicles 7:14)

4. *For Protection from Evil:* Prayer shields the nation from disasters, terrorism, and moral decay. (Psalm 91:1-2)

5. *For Economic and Social Prosperity:* God blesses nations that seek Him. (Psalm 33:12)

How to Pray for the Nation

1. *Pray for Leaders:* Lift up the king, the president, governors, ministers, and all decision-makers to God for wisdom, integrity, and guidance.

2. *Pray for Righteous Laws:* Ask God to establish laws that reflect His justice and moral standards.

3. *Pray for National Unity:* Intercede against division, strife, and hatred, praying for love and reconciliation.

4. *Pray for the Church's Role:* Seek revival in the Church so that believers shine as lights and impact society.

5. *Pray for National Protection:* Ask for divine protection against external and internal threats.

Biblical Examples of National Prayers

- *Abraham Interceded for Sodom* (*Genesis 18:22-33*) Abraham pleaded for God's mercy upon a sinful city, demonstrating the power of intercession.

- *Moses Prayed for Israel* (*Exodus 32:11-14*) Moses stood in the gap, asking God to spare Israel despite their rebellion.

- **Daniel's Prayer for His Nation** (*Daniel 9:3-19*) Daniel repented on behalf of Israel, seeking God's forgiveness and restoration.

- **Nehemiah's Prayer for Jerusalem** (*Nehemiah 1:4-11*) Nehemiah's intercession led to the rebuilding of Jerusalem's walls.

A Model Prayer for the Nation

Heavenly Father, we come before You in humility, lifting up our nation before Your throne. Your Word instructs us to pray for those in authority, so we ask for wisdom, integrity, and righteousness to govern our leaders. Let Your justice prevail in our land, and may our laws reflect Your truth. Heal our nation of division, strife, and corruption. Pour out Your Spirit upon us, bringing revival and awakening. Protect us from every form of evil, disaster, and attack. Let Your Kingdom come, and Your Will be done in our land. In Jesus' name, Amen.

Prayer for the nation is not just an option; it is a biblical duty. When believers intercede fervently, God moves powerfully. Through prayer, nations can experience transformation, healing, and divine intervention. Let us commit to standing in the gap for our land, trusting that God will hear and answer our prayers.

52

PRAYER FOR LEADERS AND AUTHORITIES
(PROVERBS 21:1)

"The king's heart is in the hand of the Lord, as the rivers of water:
He turneth it whithersoever He will."

Leaders and authorities play a crucial role in shaping societies, churches, and nations. Whether in government, business, or spiritual leadership, their decisions impact many lives. As believers, we are called to pray for those in authority so that they may lead with wisdom, righteousness, and a heart aligned with God's will.

The Bible repeatedly emphasizes the importance of praying for leaders. Paul exhorted Timothy, saying:

"I exhort therefore, that, first of all, supplications, prayers, intercessions, and giving of thanks, be made for all men; for kings, and for all that are in authority; that we may lead a quiet and peaceable life in all Godliness and honesty." (1 Timothy 2:1-2)

Our prayers can influence the decisions of leaders, guide their hearts toward justice, and establish Godly governance in every sphere of life.

Why Pray for Leaders and Authorities?

To Align Their Hearts with God's Will

Proverbs 21:1 reminds us that God has the power to direct the hearts of leaders. Through prayer, we invite God to influence their decisions and actions.

For Wisdom and Understanding

Leaders face complex decisions that require divine wisdom. James 1:5 encourages us to ask God for wisdom, and He gives it generously.

For Righteousness and Justice to Prevail

Proverbs 29:2 states, *"When the righteous are in authority, the people rejoice: but when the wicked beareth rule, the people mourn."* Prayer can help establish righteous leadership that benefits the people.

For Protection Against Corruption and Deception

The enemy seeks to corrupt leaders and derail them from fulfilling God's purpose. Ephesians 6:12 reminds us that *we wrestle against spiritual wickedness in high places*.

For Peace and Stability in Nations and Churches

When leaders govern righteously, societies experience peace. Praying for them contributes to a stable and flourishing community (Jeremiah 29:7).

How to Pray for Leaders and Authorities

Pray for Their Hearts to be Yielded to God

Father, turn the hearts of our leaders to You. Let them seek Your wisdom in their decisions (Proverbs 21:1).

Pray for Divine Wisdom and Understanding

Lord, grant our leaders wisdom, knowledge, and discernment to lead justly and righteously (James 1:5).

Pray for Righteousness and Integrity

Heavenly Father, raise up leaders who fear You and uphold justice. Let righteousness prevail in governance (Proverbs 29:2).

Pray Against Corruption and Unrighteous Influences

Lord, expose and remove every corrupt influence over our leaders. Protect them from deception and evil counsel (Ephesians 6:12).

Pray for National Peace and Prosperity

Father, through Godly leadership, let our nation experience peace, stability, and progress (Jeremiah 29:7).

Pray for Church and Ministry Leaders

Lord, strengthen pastors and spiritual leaders. Give them grace to shepherd Your people in truth and love (Hebrews 13:17).

Biblical Examples of Prayers for Leaders

Daniel's Intercession for kings

Daniel served under various kings and continually prayed for them. In Daniel 6:10, he remained faithful in prayer despite opposition.

Nehemiah's Prayer for the king's Favor

Nehemiah prayed for king Artaxerxes, and God moved the king's heart to support the rebuilding of Jerusalem (Nehemiah 1:11; 2:4-8).

Moses' Intercession for Israel's Leaders

Moses frequently interceded for Israel's leaders, seeking God's mercy and guidance (Exodus 32:11-14).

Praying for leaders and authorities is a biblical mandate with powerful results. As we intercede for those in leadership, we invite God's guidance, wisdom, and righteousness into our communities, churches, and nations. Let us commit to lifting up our leaders daily so that they may govern with integrity and lead according to God's perfect will.

Prayer Declaration:

Heavenly Father, we lift up our leaders before You. We ask that You guide their hearts, direct their decisions, and fill them with wisdom. Let righteousness and justice prevail in our nation and among those in authority. Protect them from corruption and evil counsel. Let Your will be done in their lives and through their leadership, in Jesus' name. Amen!

53

PRAYER FOR JUSTICE AND RIGHTEOUSNESS
(AMOS 5:24)

"But let judgment run down as waters,
and righteousness as a mighty stream."

Justice and righteousness are foundational to God's Kingdom. He is a God of justice, and He calls His people to reflect His heart by upholding truth, fairness, and righteousness in society. The prophet Amos, addressing the injustices of his time, declared God's desire for justice to flow abundantly rather than empty religious practices. As believers, we are called to intercede for justice to prevail in our communities, nations, and the world.

The Need for Justice and Righteousness

The world is filled with oppression, corruption, and inequality. The poor, the weak, and the marginalized often suffer under unjust systems. As followers of Christ, we cannot be passive; we must pray and take action to see God's righteousness manifest.

259 Prayer for Justice and Righteousness

Through prayer, we invite God's justice into situations of unfairness and ask Him to bring restoration.

Key Aspects of Praying for Justice and Righteousness

1. Praying for Leaders and Authorities

The Bible instructs us to pray for those in authority (1 Timothy 2:1-2). We should ask God to raise leaders who uphold justice and remove those who promote oppression.

Prayer:

Father, we lift up our leaders before You. Give them wisdom to govern with righteousness and fairness. Let them defend the rights of the poor and needy. Expose corruption and replace wicked rulers with those who fear You in Jesus' name, Amen.

2. Praying Against Injustice and Oppression

God commands us to stand against oppression. We should pray for the breaking of unjust systems that harm people.

Prayer:

Lord, let the cries of the oppressed reach You. Arise and defend the helpless. Break the strongholds of injustice, and let Your righteousness be established in every land. We declare freedom for those bound by unfair policies and structures in Jesus' name, Amen.

3. Praying for the Church to Be a Voice of Justice

The Church must be a voice of justice. It should not be silent in the face of wrongdoing but should advocate for righteousness *in Jesus' name, Amen.*

Prayer:

Lord, awaken Your Church to stand boldly for truth and justice. Let believers be Your hands and feet, ministering to the broken and challenging injustice wherever it is found in Jesus' name, Amen.

4. Praying for Personal Righteousness

Justice begins in our hearts. We must ask God to make us people of integrity who live out His righteousness in our daily lives.

Prayer:

Father, purify my heart. Help me to walk in Your righteousness and be an example of justice. Let my actions reflect Your love and fairness to all I encounter in Jesus' name, Amen.

Biblical Examples of Prayers for Justice

- *Abraham Interceding for Sodom* (*Genesis 18:23-33*) Abraham pleaded for the righteous to be spared from destruction.
- *The Persistent Widow* (*Luke 18:1-8*) Jesus Christ illustrated the power of persistent prayer for justice through a widow who kept seeking justice from an unrighteous judge.

Praying for justice and righteousness is essential in the world. As we lift our voices in intercession, we align with God's will and invite His divine intervention. May we be faithful in seeking justice, living righteously, and reflecting God's heart to the world.

54

PRAYER FOR PEACE IN TROUBLED LANDS
(PSALM 122:6)

"Pray for the peace of Jerusalem:
May they prosper who love you."

The Need for Peace in Troubled Lands

We live in a world where conflicts, wars, and unrest have devastated some nations, communities, and families. From political instability to religious persecution, economic hardship, and violence, many regions suffer under the weight of turmoil. The Bible calls us to be intercessors, standing in the gap for these troubled lands and crying out for God's peace. As believers, we have a divine mandate to pray for the peace of our cities, nations, and the world at large (Jeremiah 29:7).

Peace is not just the absence of war; it is the presence of God's righteousness, justice, and harmony. True peace can only be established when the Prince of Peace, Jesus Christ, reigns in the hearts of men and women. Our prayers can shift atmospheres, break chains of oppression, and invite the Spirit of peace to reign in places of distress.

Biblical Examples of Praying for Peace

Throughout Scripture, we see Godly men and women interceding for their nations. Abraham pleaded for Sodom and Gomorrah (Genesis 18:23-32), Moses stood in the gap for Israel (Exodus 32:11-14), and Daniel prayed earnestly for the restoration of his people (Daniel 9:3-19). The Psalmist specifically calls us to pray for Jerusalem, recognizing that peace in the land of God's people brings blessings to those who love it.

Jesus Christ, before the crucifixion, wept over Jerusalem, lamenting its rejection of peace (Luke 19:41-44). His example teaches us that prayer for troubled lands is not just a duty but an expression of deep compassion and concern.

How to Pray for Peace in Troubled Lands

Pray for God's Intervention: Ask the Lord to intervene in regions affected by war, violence, and unrest. Pray that His sovereign hand would bring order where there is chaos.

Pray for Leaders: Lift up national and community leaders, that they may govern with wisdom, righteousness, and justice (1 Timothy 2:1-2).

Pray for Protection of the Innocent: Intercede for civilians, especially children, widows, and refugees, that God may shield them from harm (Psalm 91:1-4).

Pray for Healing and Reconciliation: Ask God to heal the wounds of conflict, bring reconciliation among warring factions, and restore broken relationships (2 Chronicles 7:14).

Pray for the Gospel to Spread: Where there is war and destruction, people need the hope of Christ. Pray that the light of the Gospel will shine in dark places (Isaiah 9:2).

A Sample Prayer for Peace

Heavenly Father, we lift up the nations and lands that are troubled by war, violence, and unrest. Your Word commands us to pray for the peace of Jerusalem and to seek the welfare of the lands where You have placed us. Lord, we ask for Your divine intervention in every place torn by conflict. Stretch forth Your mighty hand and bring an end to destruction and bloodshed.

We pray for the leaders of nations, that they may rule with wisdom, justice, and righteousness. Give them hearts of compassion and minds led by Your Spirit. Protect the innocent, O Lord. Shield the vulnerable, and provide for those who have lost homes, and security. Let Your healing flow through these lands, restoring what has been broken and torn apart.

Father, we pray for unity and reconciliation among communities divided by hatred. Let forgiveness and understanding replace bitterness and revenge. May Your peace, which surpasses all understanding, guard the hearts and minds of those who dwell in these regions. Above all, let Your Kingdom come and Your will be done on earth as it is in Heaven.

In Jesus' name, we pray. Amen.

The Promise of Peace

God assures us that He hears and answers the prayers of the righteous (James 5:16). As we continually intercede for troubled lands, we trust in His promise that the Prince of Peace will establish His Kingdom where war will cease, and His righteousness will reign (Isaiah 2:4, Revelation 21:4). Until that day, let us remain faithful in our prayers, knowing that our intercession makes a difference.

55

PRAYER FOR ECONOMIC PROSPERITY
(DEUTERONOMY 28:12)

Economic prosperity is a blessing that comes from God when we align our lives with His principles. Deuteronomy 28:12 declares, *"The Lord will open to you His good treasure, the heavens, to give the rain to your land in its season, and to bless all the work of your hand. You shall lend to many nations, but you shall not borrow."* This verse reveals God's desire for His people to walk in financial abundance so they can be a blessing to others.

Understanding Economic Prosperity in God's Kingdom

True economic prosperity goes beyond material wealth; it includes peace, sufficiency, and the ability to give generously. The Bible teaches that prosperity follows obedience (Deuteronomy 28:1-2). It is not just about financial gain but about being a steward of God's resources.

God as the Source: Recognizing that wealth and provision come from God, (Deuteronomy 8:18) ensures that we do not rely on our own strength but trust in Him.

Diligence and Hard Work: Proverbs 10:4 says, *"He who has a slack hand becomes poor, But the hand of the diligent makes rich."* God blesses those who work hard and apply wisdom in their finances.

Tithing and Giving: Malachi 3:10-12 speaks of bringing the tithe into God's house, and He promises to open the windows of Heaven and many blessings.

Wise Stewardship: Avoiding debt, investing wisely, and budgeting responsibly align with biblical principles of financial management.

Generosity: Proverbs 11:25 teaches, *"A generous person will prosper; whoever refreshes others will be refreshed."* Giving is a key to sustained financial blessings.

Praying for Economic Prosperity

When we pray for financial prosperity, we should approach God with faith, obedience, and a heart ready to bless others. Here is a powerful prayer for economic prosperity:

Prayer:

Heavenly Father, I thank You for being my provider and my source. Your Word in Deuteronomy 28:12 promises that You will bless the work of my hands and make me a lender, not a borrower. Lord, I surrender my finances to You and ask for wisdom in managing the resources You entrust to me.

I pray for divine opportunities, creative ideas, and open doors that will lead to financial breakthroughs. Let the heavens be open over my life, and pour out blessings in due season. I reject every form of lack, debt, and financial mismanagement. Teach me to honor You with my wealth through tithing, giving, and wise investments.

Father, I declare that I am blessed in my business, my career, and all my endeavors. May everything I touch prosper according to Your will. Remove any hindrance to my financial growth, and establish me in abundance so that I can be a blessing to others. I decree and declare that my finances align with Kingdom principles, and I will walk in supernatural provision, in Jesus' name. Amen.

Applying Faith and Action

Prayer must be accompanied by action. Here are practical steps to walk in economic prosperity:

1. *Confess God's Promises Daily:* Speak life over your finances using Scriptures such as Philippians 4:19, *"My God shall supply all my needs according to His riches in glory."*

2. *Develop Financial Discipline:* Budget wisely, avoid unnecessary debt, and save diligently.

3. *Invest in Knowledge:* Learn financial principles and seek God's guidance in decision-making.

4. *Engage in Productive Work:* Whether in business, employment, or ministry, work with excellence and integrity.

5. *Give and Bless Others:* Support the needy, sow into God's work, and maintain a generous spirit.

God desires His children to prosper, not for selfish gain, but to advance His Kingdom and bless others. By praying, applying biblical principles, and working diligently, we position ourselves to receive His financial blessings. As you trust in God's provision, walk in obedience, and seek wisdom, He will establish you in economic prosperity according to His perfect plan.

L

PRAYERS FOR EVANGELISM AND MISSIONS

56

PRAYER FOR OPEN DOORS FOR THE GOSPEL
(COLOSSIANS 4:3)

*"Meanwhile praying also for us, that God would open to us
a door for the word, to speak the mystery of Christ,
for which I am also in chains."*

The Need for Open Doors in the Gospel Mission

The spread of the Gospel requires divine intervention. Paul, as an apostle, understood the necessity of prayer in securing open doors for the Word of God. He urged the Colossian believers to pray specifically that God would create opportunities for the message of Christ to be proclaimed. This brings an essential principle: Evangelism is not just a human endeavor but a work that must be empowered by God.

When we pray for open doors for the Gospel, we acknowledge our dependence on God to remove barriers, soften hearts, and grant favor before those who need salvation. Many times, spiritual and physical obstacles hinder the proclamation of truth.

These barriers can be political restrictions, cultural opposition, hardened hearts, or logistical difficulties. But through fervent prayer, we invite divine intervention to make a way where there seems to be none.

Biblical Examples of Open Doors

Throughout the Bible, we see examples of God opening doors for the Gospel:

Paul's Macedonian Call (Acts 16:9-10). God directed Paul through a vision to go to Macedonia, where the Gospel was needed.

Peter and Cornelius (Acts 10:1-48). God orchestrated an encounter between Peter and a Gentile centurion, breaking traditional barriers for the Gospel.

Philip and the Ethiopian Eunuch (Acts 8:26-40). The Spirit led Philip to a man seeking the truth, resulting in his conversion.

Each of these instances reminds us that God is actively involved in missions and evangelism, and our prayers align us with His divine plan.

How to Pray for Open Doors

Pray for Divine Appointments: Ask God to connect you with those He has prepared to receive His Word.

1. *Pray Against Opposition:* Intercede against spiritual and human resistance to the Gospel.

2. *Pray for Boldness:* Like Paul, pray for courage to proclaim the truth despite challenges.

3. *Pray for Receptive Hearts:* Ask that those who hear the Word will be convicted and respond in faith.

4. *Pray for Favor:* That authorities, institutions, and communities will welcome the Gospel message.

A Prayer for Open Doors

Heavenly Father,

Thank You for calling us to be bearers of Your Good News. Just as Paul sought the prayers of the saints for open doors, we ask that You open doors for the Gospel in our time. Remove every hindrance; whether spiritual, political, or personal, that stands in the way of Your Word reaching those in darkness.

Lord, prepare the hearts of those who will hear the message of salvation. Soften their hearts, remove blindness, and let the light of Christ shine upon them. Grant us boldness, wisdom, and the anointing of the Holy Spirit to speak Your Word with power and clarity. May we find favor with people in positions of influence so that Your Gospel may go forth unhindered.

We declare that nations, communities, and hearts will be opened to Your truth. Use us as vessels to spread Your Word effectively. In Jesus' name, Amen.

Prayer for open doors is crucial for the advancement of God's Kingdom. As believers, we must continually intercede, trusting that God will remove barriers and prepare the way for His Word. Through prayer, we become co-laborers with Christ, ensuring that the Gospel reaches every corner of the earth. Let us, therefore, persist in seeking open doors, knowing that God is faithful to answer.

"The Lord opens doors no man can shut" (Revelation 3:8). Keep praying, keep believing, and keep proclaiming!

57

PRAYER FOR BOLDNESS IN WITNESSING
(ACTS 4:29)

*"Now, Lord, look on their threats, and grant to Your servants
that with all boldness they may speak Your word."*

The Need for Boldness in Witnessing

Witnessing for Christ is an essential part of the Christian faith. Jesus commissioned His disciples to go into all the world and preach the gospel (Mark 16:15). However, many believers face challenges such as fear, intimidation, and opposition. In Acts 4:29, the early Church encountered threats, yet they prayed for boldness rather than retreating in fear. This prayer remains relevant today.

Biblical Examples of Boldness in Witnessing

Peter and John Before the Sanhedrin (Acts 4:13-20): Despite being commanded not to speak in Jesus' name, they declared they could not remain silent.

Paul in Corinth (Acts 18:9-10): The Lord reassured Paul not to be afraid but to keep speaking.

Daniel in Babylon (Daniel 6:10-23): Despite the king's decree, Daniel continued his prayers openly, demonstrating unwavering faith.

Overcoming Fear with Prayer

Fear is one of the greatest obstacles to witnessing. The early believers understood that without divine empowerment, they would be ineffective. Their response was to pray, and God answered by filling them with the Holy Spirit (Acts 4:31). Prayer for boldness involves asking God to:

• Remove fear and hesitation.
• Fill us with the Holy Spirit.
• Give us the right words to speak (Luke 12:12).
• Strengthen us in the face of opposition.

Characteristics of Bold Witnesses

Confidence in God's Word: They believe in the power of the Gospel (Romans 1:16).

Unshaken by Opposition: They are willing to suffer for Christ (2 Timothy 1:7-8).

Led by the Holy Spirit: Their words carry divine authority (Acts 6:10).

Persistent in Prayer: They rely on God for strength (Ephesians 6:19-20).

Compelled by Love: Their motivation is to see souls saved (2 Corinthians 5:14-15).

A Prayer for Boldness in Witnessing

Heavenly Father, I come before You today, acknowledging my need for Your strength and courage. Lord, just as the early disciples prayed, I ask You to grant me boldness to share Your Word fearlessly. Remove every fear, doubt, and hesitation from my heart. Fill me with the Holy Spirit, that I may speak with wisdom, grace, and power. Let my words be seasoned with love and truth, drawing many to You. Strengthen me to stand firm in the face of opposition, knowing that You are with me. In Jesus' name, Amen.

Boldness in witnessing is not a natural trait but a divine empowerment that comes through prayer. The more we seek God, the more we are filled with His Spirit, emboldened to proclaim His truth without fear. Let us make this prayer a daily part of our lives, trusting God to use us mightily for His Kingdom.

58

PRAYER FOR SOULS TO BE SAVED
(1 TIMOTHY 2:4)

*"Who desires all men to be saved
and to come to the knowledge of the truth."*

God's greatest desire is for souls to be saved. Salvation is at the very heart of His plan for humanity. Every believer has a divine mandate to pray for the salvation of souls, interceding that the lost would turn to Christ and be delivered from the kingdom of darkness into the Kingdom of light. This is not just an option; it is a responsibility entrusted to us by God.

The Need for Salvation

Sin separates humanity from God, and without Christ, people remain lost. Romans 3:23 reminds us, *"For all have sinned and fall short of the Glory of God."* However, through the redemptive work of Christ, salvation has been made available to all who believe. Jesus said in John 14:6, *"I am the way, the truth, and the life. No one comes to* the *Father except through Me.*" This means that prayer for the lost is essential in bringing them to the knowledge of the truth.

Biblical Examples of Praying for the Lost

The Bible provides several examples of intercessory prayers for salvation. One of the most striking examples is Abraham's intercession for Sodom in Genesis 18:23-33. Though the city was filled with wickedness, Abraham stood in the gap, pleading for mercy. Similarly, Paul expressed his deep burden for the salvation of Israel in Romans 10:1: *"Brethren, my heart's desire and prayer to God for Israel is that they may be saved."* This shows us that persistent, fervent prayer can play a crucial role in leading people to Christ.

How to Pray for Souls to Be Saved

Pray for Their Hearts to Be Opened: Ask God to remove spiritual blindness and open their hearts to the gospel. (2 Corinthians 4:4)

Pray for Laborers in the Harvest: Jesus instructed us to pray for laborers who will preach the Word effectively. (Matthew 9:37-38)

Pray for Conviction by the Holy Spirit: The Holy Spirit convicts people of sin, righteousness, and judgment. (John 16:8)

Pray for Divine Appointments: Ask God to orchestrate circumstances that will draw them to salvation. (Acts 8:26-40)

Pray for Their Deliverance from the Power of Darkness: Many souls are bound by the enemy. Pray for their spiritual freedom. (Colossians 1:13)

The Role of the Church in Soul-Winning Prayer

The Church must be committed to corporate prayer for salvation. In Acts 12, the early church gathered to pray for Peter's release, demonstrating the power of united intercession. When believers join together to pray for souls, God moves mightily. Churches should set aside specific times to pray for the lost, organize evangelistic prayer meetings, and encourage believers to maintain a lifestyle of intercessory prayer for the unsaved.

A Model Prayer for Souls to Be Saved

Heavenly Father,

We thank You for Your love and mercy, and we acknowledge that it is Your desire that all men be saved and come to the knowledge of the truth. We lift up those who are lost, asking that You would open their hearts to receive Your Word. Remove every veil of deception and every stronghold that keeps them from knowing You. Send laborers across their paths to share the message of salvation. Holy Spirit, convict them of sin, righteousness, and judgment, and draw them into a personal relationship with Jesus Christ. We declare that the enemy's grip over their lives is broken, and they will experience the joy of Salvation. In Jesus' name, Amen.

Praying for souls to be saved is one of the most important prayers a believer can offer. As we intercede, we partner with God in His redemptive plan. May we never grow weary in this divine assignment, knowing that every soul brought into the Kingdom is a victory for Christ. *"The fruit of the righteous is a tree of life, and he who wins souls is wise."* Proverbs 11:30.

59

PRAYER FOR LABORERS IN THE HARVEST
(MATTHEW 9:37-38)

"Then He said to His disciples, 'The harvest truly is plentiful, but the laborers are few. Therefore, pray the Lord of the harvest to send out laborers into His harvest.'"

The Call for Laborers

The words of Jesus Christ in Matthew 9:37-38 show a critical need in the Kingdom of God: the need for laborers in the harvest field. The harvest represents the souls of men and women who are ready to receive the Gospel, but without workers to bring in the harvest, many remain lost. Jesus does not command His disciples to simply go out; instead, He first calls them to pray to the Lord of the harvest to send laborers. This emphasizes that the work of evangelism and ministry begins with prayer.

Understanding the Need for Prayer

The need for more laborers is not just about numbers but about readiness, willingness, and divine commissioning. Many people are lost, and though the Gospel message is available, there is a shortage of dedicated workers to take the message to them. The Church must rise in prayer to call forth more people who are equipped, anointed, and prepared to serve in God's vineyard.

The Harvest is Plentiful: The world is full of people searching for hope, truth, and salvation. Many are ready to turn to God if only someone would reach them with the message of Christ.

The Laborers are Few: Though many profess to be Christians, few are actively engaged in soul-winning and Kingdom work.

The Lord of the Harvest Sends the Laborers: It is God who calls, equips, and sends His workers. Our responsibility is to pray for His divine sending and empowering of laborers.

How to Pray for Laborers

Praying for laborers means interceding for God to raise up willing and faithful servants who will take the Gospel to the ends of the earth. Here are some key areas to focus on:

Pray for Willing Hearts: Ask God to touch the hearts of believers to be willing to serve in His vineyard (Isaiah 6:8).

Pray for Divine Calling: Ask the Lord to call people into specific ministries, whether in local churches, missionary work, or evangelistic outreach.

Pray for Boldness and Strength: Many hesitate due to fear, uncertainty, or personal limitations. Pray for courage and boldness (Acts 4:29).

Pray for Spiritual Equipping: Laborers need wisdom, discernment, and the power of the Holy Spirit (Luke 24:49).

Pray for Open Doors: Opportunities for ministry must be divinely arranged so that the right people reach the right places (Colossians 4:3).

Pray for Endurance and Commitment: The work is not always easy, and many become weary. Pray for strength to remain steadfast (Galatians 6:9).

Biblical Examples of Laborers in the Harvest

- *Jesus Christ Himself*: The ultimate laborer who came to seek and save the lost (Luke 19:10).

- *The Apostles*: They responded to Jesus' call and spread the Gospel despite great opposition (Acts 1:8).

- *Paul and His Missionary Team*: They labored in many regions, planting churches and making disciples (Romans 15:19-20).

The work of evangelism is urgent, and the need for laborers remains great. As we obey The Lord Jesus' command to pray for laborers, we should also be willing to be used by God in whatever capacity He calls us. May our prayers stir up a new generation of dedicated Kingdom workers who will bring in the great harvest for God's glory.

60

PRAYER FOR SIGNS AND WONDERS IN EVANGELISM
(MARK 16:20)

"And they went forth, and preached every where,
the Lord working with them, and confirming the word
with signs following. Amen."

The Role of Signs and Wonders in Evangelism

Evangelism is not only about words; it is a demonstration of the power of God. Jesus sent His disciples into the world to preach the Gospel, but He did not leave them without evidence of His divine backing. He confirmed their message with signs and wonders. In the same way, we must pray for the supernatural manifestation of God's power to accompany our evangelistic efforts. Signs and wonders serve as undeniable proof of God's presence, turning hearts towards Him.

Biblical Examples of Signs and Wonders in Evangelism

Jesus Christ: The Lord performed many miracles, healing the sick, casting out demons, and raising the dead, drawing multitudes to God (John 20:30-31).

The Apostles: In the Book of Acts, the early church experienced the power of God through healings, deliverances, and miraculous interventions (Acts 5:12-16).

Philip in Samaria: When Philip preached in Samaria, people believed because of the signs and miracles God performed through him (Acts 8:6-8).

Paul's Ministry: Paul boldly preached the Gospel, and God confirmed it with signs, causing both Jews and Gentiles to believe (Romans 15:18-19).

Why We Must Pray for Signs and Wonders

To Glorify God: Miracles reveal God's power and bring glory to His name (John 11:40).

To Validate the Gospel: Unbelievers are drawn to the truth when they see undeniable evidence of God's power (Acts 14:3).

To Break Satanic Strongholds: Signs and wonders defeat the power of darkness, setting captives free (Luke 10:19).

To Encourage the Faithful: The Church is strengthened when believers witness God's power at work (Acts 4:29-30).

How to Pray for Signs and Wonders in Evangelism

Pray for Boldness: Ask God to grant you courage to preach His word without fear (Acts 4:29).

Pray for God's Presence: Signs and wonders happen when God is actively working through His people (Exodus 33:15-16).

Pray for Faith: Believe in the miraculous power of God and expect Him to move (Mark 9:23).

Pray for the Gifts of the Spirit: Healing, prophecy, and miracles operate through the Holy Spirit (1 Corinthians 12:8-10).

Pray for an Open Heaven: Ask God to open the spiritual realm so that His power flows freely (Isaiah 64:1-2).

A Prayer for Signs and Wonders in Evangelism

Heavenly Father, I thank You for calling me to preach the Gospel and be a witness of Your glory. Lord, I pray that as I go forth, You will confirm Your word with signs and wonders. Stretch out Your hand to heal the sick, deliver the oppressed, and perform miracles that will bring glory to Your name. Let Your power be evident so that many will believe in Jesus Christ. Fill me with boldness, faith, and the gifts of the Holy Spirit to be an effective vessel for Your Kingdom. I surrender to You, Lord. Work through me for Your glory. In Jesus' name, Amen!

Signs and wonders are a divine tool for evangelism. When we pray and step out in faith, God moves in extraordinary ways to bring people into His Kingdom. Let us desire and seek His power so that our evangelism is not just in words but in demonstration of the Spirit and power (1 Corinthians 2:4-5).

M

PRAYERS FOR SPIRITUAL GROWTH AND MATURITY

61

PRAYER FOR SPIRITUAL STRENGTH
(EPHESIANS 3:16)

"That He would grant you, according to the riches of His glory,
to be strengthened with might by His Spirit in the inner man."

In the Apostle Paul's prayer for the believers in Ephesus, we find a profound petition: not for physical needs or material blessings, but for **inner strength**. This kind of prayer touches the very core of Christian life and maturity: the inner man being fortified by the power of the Holy Spirit. It is a prayer that aligns perfectly with God's desire to see His children grow up into Christ in all things (Ephesians 4:15).

1. Understanding the "Inner Man"

The *inner man* refers to the **spiritual being** of a person; the re-generated, born-again part that communes with God. Just as the outer man (our body) needs food, rest, and strength, the inner man requires **spiritual nourishment** and **divine empowerment**.

Paul's prayer is that God, out of the abundance of His glory, would infuse power into this inner person.

Spiritual strength doesn't come by self-discipline or sheer willpower; it is a gift of grace that flows from the Holy Spirit. We do not fight spiritual battles with fleshly weapons; we fight in the strength He provides (2 Corinthians 10:3-5). When we are strengthened in the inner man, we are able to stand firm in trials, resist temptation, and walk in victory.

2. Strength "According to the Riches of His Glory"

Paul ask God to give us strength *according to* His riches. This is a huge difference. If a billionaire gives out of his wealth, he may give a hundred euros. But if he gives according to his wealth, it could be millions. Paul is pointing to the unlimited resources of God's glory as the measure by which we are to be strengthened.

God's glory is not weak. It is majestic, weighty, and full of power. It is the very atmosphere of heaven and the manifestation of all that God is. When God strengthens us according to His glory, we are filled with divine capacity beyond human limitation.

3. Strengthened with Might by His Spirit

The Greek word for *might* in this verse is **"dunamis"**, from which we get the word "dynamite." It refers to explosive, miraculous power. This is not ordinary strength; it is supernatural ability given by the Holy Spirit. He imparts this might not just to help us cope, but to thrive, overcome, and carry out God's will on earth.

This power:

- Enables us to say "no" to sin (Romans 8:13),
- Helps us pray when we are weak (Romans 8:26),
- Produces the fruit of the Spirit in us (Galatians 5:22-23),
- And gives us boldness to witness (Acts 1:8).

When we pray for spiritual strength, we are asking the Holy Spirit to actively work in us; not just to visit us, but to dwell, to renew, and to energize us.

4. Why We Need This Kind of Prayer

Many believers are spiritually tired; not because they lack the will to serve God, but because they lack **inner strength**. They may be faithful in church, diligent in service, yet feel dry and weary. Paul, a seasoned apostle, knew that for believers to live victoriously, their **inner man must be constantly renewed** (2 Corinthians 4:16).

This prayer is crucial because:

- We face *daily spiritual battles* (Ephesians 6:12).
- We need *endurance* for the Christian race (Hebrews 12:1-3).
- We are called to *grow into the fullness of Christ* (Ephesians 4:13).
- We are not called to live in our own strength, but in *God's divine enablement.*

This is not a one-time prayer but a **daily pursuit**. Just as our physical bodies weaken without food or exercise, our spirits need the **continual strengthening work of the Holy Spirit.**

5. How to Pray for Spiritual Strength

You can personalize Ephesians 3:16 into a powerful, daily prayer. Let it shape your inner life. Here is an example:

"Heavenly Father, I pray that You would strengthen me with might through Your Holy Spirit in my inner man. According to the riches of Your glory, fill me with Your divine energy. Let my spirit be empowered to do Your will, to resist the enemy, and to walk in the fullness of Your purpose for my life. In Jesus' name."

You can also pray this for others, family members, pastors, church workers, or new believers.

Consider praying:

"Lord, strengthen my brothers/sisters in their inner beings. Empower them with divine might. Let Your Holy Spirit flood their souls with courage, peace, and resilience. Renew their hearts, give them endurance, and let them walk in joy and power. In Jesus' name."

Praying this way helps us move beyond surface-level prayers and into the heart of intercession. We are not only praying for comfort or material breakthrough, but for transformation from the inside out.

6. Signs You Are Strengthened in the Inner Man

When your inner man is strong, certain things begin to manifest:

- You are more stable emotionally and spiritually.
- You are not easily offended or discouraged.

- You face challenges with confidence in God's promises.
- You grow in love, faith, and holiness.
- You become a source of encouragement to others.

This kind of strength enables you to carry spiritual responsibility without burning out. You are able to lead, to intercede, to labor in ministry, not in your own ability, but in the sufficiency of the Spirit.

62

PRAYER FOR GREATER KNOWLEDGE OF GOD
(COLOSSIANS 1:9-10)

"For this cause we also, since the day we heard it,
do not cease to pray for you, and to desire that ye might be filled
with the knowledge of His will in all wisdom and spiritual understanding;
¹⁰ That ye might walk worthy of the Lord unto all pleasing,
being fruitful in every good work, and increasing in the knowledge of God."

The Prayer for Knowledge of God

One of the deepest cries of the human heart, whether knowingly or unknowingly, is to understand the divine: to know God. When Paul wrote to the believers in Colossae, he highlighted this as a central point of his continuous prayers for them: that they would grow in the knowledge of God. This kind of knowledge is not superficial or theoretical, but deeply experiential and transformational. It is knowledge that matures us spiritually and aligns us with the perfect Will of God.

Spiritual growth cannot occur outside of the knowledge of God. As a plant needs sunlight to grow, so does the believer need divine light; the knowledge of God to mature and bear fruit. The more we know Him, the more we reflect Him. The more we understand His will, the more our lives are lived in alignment with His purpose.

What It Means to "Know" God

In the Bible, to "know" someone often means more than having information about them. It is relational and personal. It goes beyond surface understanding and suggests a deep, spiritual comprehension that affects the heart and the walk of the believer.

This prayer is not simply about acquiring more Bible facts or theological insights. Rather, it is about experiencing God through a relationship that is nourished by the Holy Spirit. It is the kind of knowledge that transforms us from the inside out.

The Role of the Holy Spirit in Knowing God

Paul acknowledges that this knowledge comes through "all spiritual wisdom and understanding," which is granted by the Holy Spirit. The Spirit of God is our Divine Teacher. He reveals Christ to us, opens our eyes to the Scriptures, and brings illumination where there was once darkness.

This is why prayer is essential. We do not grow in the knowledge of God just by academic study. Prayer invites the Holy Spirit to open our hearts and minds, to teach us the things of God. It is through prayer that revelation flows. As it is written in 1

Corinthians 2:10, *"These are the things God has revealed to us by His Spirit. The Spirit searches all things, even the deep things of God."*

When we pray for the knowledge of God, we are humbling ourselves and acknowledging that our intellect is limited, and only God can grant us the understanding we need to walk in His will.

Why This Prayer Matters Today

In today's busy world, believers can become preoccupied with knowledge that does not profit the soul. Social media, endless news cycles, worldly trends; all these can fill the mind, yet leave the heart empty. This is why the prayer in Colossians 1:9-10 is so important. It helps us refocus our attention on what truly matters: knowing God and walking in a way that pleases Him.

The prayer for the knowledge of God is not about puffing up the mind but building up the spirit. It is knowledge that leads to action, fruitfulness, and a deeper relationship with the Father.

Living a Life Worthy of the Lord

Paul's prayer continues in verse 10, explaining the result of this knowledge: *"so that you may live a life worthy of the Lord and please Him in every way."* This is a high calling. It means that knowing God should affect the way we live, speak, serve, give, and love.

Knowledge of God is not an end in itself; it is a means to a transformed life. When we truly know Who God is: His holiness, His justice, His mercy, His faithfulness, we begin to live in awe of Him. Our lives begin to reflect His character. We become more obedient, more loving, and more fruitful.

Living a life that pleases God becomes our desire, not out of religious obligation, but out of love and intimacy with Him.

Bearing Fruit in Every Good Work

The next result of knowing God is *"bearing fruit in every good work."* Fruitfulness is evidence of spiritual growth. Just as a tree bears fruit when nourished properly, a believer who feeds on the knowledge of God will naturally bear spiritual fruit: love, joy, peace, patience, kindness, goodness, faithfulness, gentleness, and self-control (Galatians 5:22-23).

This fruit is not just an internal character; it also manifests in good works; acts of service, compassion, generosity, and ministry. These are not done to earn favor with God, but as a response to knowing Him deeply. A true knowledge of God leads to a life that reflects His heart to the world.

How to Pray This Kind of Prayer

Praying for the knowledge of God is not a one-time request. It is a continual posture. Just as Paul said, *"we have not stopped praying for you,"* we too must keep asking for more of God. Here are some ways you can pray this prayer:

Personalize Colossians 1:9-10:

"Father, I ask You to fill me with the knowledge of Your will through all the wisdom and understanding by Your Holy Spirit. Help me live a life worthy of You, pleasing You in every way. Let me bear fruit in every good work and grow continually in the knowledge of You."

Pray it for others: Just like Paul did, pray this prayer over your church, your family, and new believers. This is a powerful intercession that aligns people's lives with God's purpose.

Use Scripture as your foundation: Combine this with other Scriptures about knowing God (e.g., Philippians 3:10, Jeremiah 9:23-24, Ephesians 1:17-18) to deepen your prayers.

Make room for listening: After praying, take time to listen. Sometimes God wants to speak directly into your heart about areas He wants to reveal more of Himself.

Stay in the Word: God reveals Himself primarily through His Word. The more you read and meditate on the Scriptures, the more you will come to know Him. Prayer and the Word work together.

A Call to the Deeper Life

This prayer is a call to go deeper. To seek God not just for what He gives, but for Who He is. It is a prayer that brings spiritual alignment, clarity, and strength. As we grow in the knowledge of God, we grow in love, power, discernment, and purpose.

Let this kind of prayer be your daily pursuit; not only for yourself, but for those around you. As the Church returns to a deeper knowledge of God, revival and transformation will naturally follow.

63

PRAYER FOR FRUITFULNESS IN THE SPIRIT
(GALATIANS 5:22-23)

"But the fruit of the Spirit is love, joy, peace, longsuffering,
gentleness, goodness, faith, meekness, temperance:
against such there is no law."

Walking in the Spirit: The Foundation of Fruitfulness

The fruit of the Spirit is not something that can be manufactured by human effort or religious works. It is the natural product of a life that abides in Christ and is filled with the Holy Spirit. When we are rooted in God's presence and the Word, and when we yield daily to the Holy Spirit, we begin to manifest His nature and character.

Prayer for fruitfulness in the Spirit is not a prayer to receive things, but to **become** the person God desires; Christlike in every way. It is a desire for inner transformation. We are not just asking for gifts or power, but for the nature of Christ to be formed in us (Galatians 4:19). True spiritual maturity is measured by how much the fruit of the Spirit is evident in our everyday life.

Love: The First and Greatest Fruit

The first fruit mentioned is *love*. This is the agape love of God; a love that is selfless, unconditional, and sacrificial. It is the highest expression of God's character. Without love, every other manifestation of spirituality becomes empty (1 Corinthians 13:1-3).

In prayer, we ask God to help us:

- Love the unlovable.
- Forgive those who hurt us.
- Serve others without expecting anything in return.

When we grow in love, we begin to see people through the eyes of God, not through judgment or offense.

Joy and Peace: The Inner Strength of the Believer

Joy and peace are not dependent on external circumstances. They are the by-products of abiding in Christ. Joy gives us strengthand peace guards our hearts in the face of anxiety (Philippians 4:7).

Our prayers for joy and peace should include:

- Rejoicing in salvation daily.
- Refusing to let bitterness, fear, or worry take root.
- Choosing thanksgiving and praise over grumbling.

"Father, fill me with joy that flows from knowing You. Let Your peace rule in my heart. Teach me to rest in Your promises."

When a believer is joyful and at peace, even in the storm, it becomes a strong witness to the world.

Longsuffering, Gentleness, Goodness: The Power of Kindness

These three fruits show how we interact with others. *Longsuffering* is the ability to endure hardship and offense without retaliation. *Gentleness* is the calm strength that shows humility, and *goodness* is moral excellence and generosity in action.

These are often tested in the context of relationships and responsibilities. In prayer, we should ask for:

- Grace to endure difficult people and situations.
- The ability to stay kind even under pressure.
- A heart to do good, especially to those in need (Galatians 6:10).

"Lord, make me patient, kind in my words, and generous in my actions. Let me reflect Your goodness in all I do."

Such qualities make us safe and trustworthy vessels in the hands of the Lord.

Faith, Meekness, and Temperance: Inner Discipline by the Spirit

Faith here speaks of faithfulness; loyalty, reliability, and consistency in our walk with God. *Meekness* is strength under control. *Temperance* is self-control: the mastery of our desires and appetites.

These fruits are especially important in leadership, family life, and ministry. Without self-control, we can damage our testimony. Without faithfulness, we cannot be trusted with responsibility. Meekness helps us remain teachable and humble.

Our prayer should be:

"Father, help me to be faithful in all things. Teach me meekness; to yield to Your will and not seek to exalt myself. Grant me temperance, so that I may walk in holiness daily."

These fruits enable us to live victoriously over the desires of the flesh and remain strong in spiritual discipline.

Cultivating the Fruit: A Daily Process in Prayer

Just as natural fruit needs time, care, pruning, and sunshine to grow, so does spiritual fruit. We must:

- Spend time daily in the Word and in the presence of God.
- Allow the Holy Spirit to correct and shape our attitudes.
- Surrender our hearts daily and invite God to work in us.

Prayer is the key to activating this process. In prayer, we yield. In prayer, we receive strength. In prayer, we cooperate with the work of the Spirit.

Here's a sample prayer for daily spiritual fruitfulness:

"Holy Spirit, I yield my soul and spirit to You. Work in me what pleases the Father. Let the fruit of love, joy, peace, longsuffering, gentleness, goodness, faith, meekness, and temperance be evident in me. I cannot bear this

fruit without abiding in You. Take away every hindrance and prune my life, so that I may bring forth more fruit for Your glory. In Jesus' name. Amen."

Results of Fruitfulness: A Life That Glorifies God

Jesus said, *"Herein is My Father Glorified, that ye bear much fruit; so shall ye be My disciples."* (John 15:8). The fruit of the Spirit is not just for our personal benefit; it is for God's Glory and for the edification of others.

People are drawn to Christ not just by powerful sermons, but by transformed lives. When a believer walks in the fruit of the Spirit, their words carry power, their prayers have weight, and their lifestyle points others to Jesus.

The Lord desires that we not only speak in tongues, prophesy, but that we become living testimonies of His nature.

"Lord, let my life bear fruits that last. May my words, thoughts, and actions reflect Jesus Christ. Help me grow in spiritual maturity, so that I may become a vessel of glory, prepared for every good work."

64

PRAYER FOR A HEART OF OBEDIENCE
(PSALM 51:10)

David's prayer in Psalm 51 reveals a soul that longs for restoration and obedience after sin. When he cried out, *"Create in me a clean heart,"* he was not just asking for forgiveness, he was praying for a transformed inner life that would yield to God in obedience.

A heart of obedience is not natural to the flesh. When we submit ourselves to God in prayer, the Holy Spirit begins a work in us that leads to genuine change. Obedience flows from a renewed heart. It is a response to God's love and mercy.

Many people want the blessings of God but are unwilling to obey Him. Yet, obedience brings peace, joy, and divine direction. Prayer is the means by which we humble ourselves and ask the Lord to work this transformation within us.

To pray for a heart of obedience is to acknowledge that we need help from heaven to walk in God's ways. This kind of prayer is a cry for divine intervention: *"Create in me."* Only God can create what does not exist. If the heart is stubborn or rebellious, He alone can replace it with a tender, responsive heart.

When we ask God to *renew a right spirit* within us, we are praying for consistency; an inner strength that does not waver with temptation or emotion. The obedient heart is not just for the moment; it is sustained by the Spirit of God day by day.

Ask yourself: Do I resist God's promptings? Do I obey Him when it's hard or when no one is watching? Let your prayer rise with sincerity. Ask Him to make you obedient in secret and in public.

Prayer Example:

"Father, in the name of Jesus, I come before You humbly today. I acknowledge that I have not always obeyed Your Word. I confess my rebellion, pride, and excuses. Forgive me, O Lord. Create in me a clean heart. Wash me and renew me with Your Spirit.

Let my heart become soft to Your will and Your instructions. Take away the stony heart and give me a heart of flesh. Renew a steadfast spirit within me. Give me the grace to obey You Lord. Let my obedience be complete and not selective.

Holy Spirit, I yield to You. Lead me into truth. Teach me to delight in God's commandments. Help me to walk in obedience as a child of God. Let obedience become my lifestyle. In Jesus' name, Amen."

Why this prayer matters

Obedience brings protection: When we follow God's instructions, we walk under His covering (Deut. 28:1-2).

Obedience brings intimacy: Jesus said, " *He who has My command-ments and keeps them, it is he who loves Me. And he who loves Me will be loved by My Father, and I will love him and manifest Myself to him.*" (John 14:21).

Obedience brings fruitfulness: Like the vine and branches (John 15), we bear fruit when we remain in Him.

Obedience is not legalism. It is love in action. When you obey God, you are saying, "I trust You more than I trust myself." You are giving Him Lordship over your life. This is what it means to live surrendered.

Declarations to speak daily

- "I have a heart that obeys the voice of the Lord."
- "I delight in God's will more than my own."
- "The Holy Spirit empowers me to walk in truth."
- "I am quick to obey and slow to resist."
- "My obedience is complete, joyful, and lasting."

Keep praying this kind of prayer. Let Psalm 51:10 become a part of your regular devotion. The obedient heart is the fertile ground where God plants His purposes.

God is raising a people who love His commandments, because their hearts are made new.

May you be among them.

SPECIAL PRAYERS FOR DIVINE INTERVENTION

65

PRAYER FOR MIRACLES
(MARK 16:17-18)

"And these signs will follow those who believe:
In My name they will cast out demons;
they will speak with new tongues; they will take up serpents;
and if they drink anything deadly, it will by no means hurt them;
they will lay hands on the sick, and they will recover."

The God we serve is a God of miracles. The Bible is filled with stories that defy human logic; water turning into wine, the blind seeing, the dead raised, the lame walking, and food multiplying. These are not fairy tales; they are signs of The living God who still works wonders today. The prayer for miracles is rooted in the power and authority of Jesus Christ. It is a faith-activated channel through which heaven touches the earth.

Jesus said clearly in Mark 16:17-18 that signs would follow those who believe; not the apostles only, but *"those who believe."* This means that every believer has access to the miraculous. The prayer for miracles acknowledges that we serve a supernatural God and invites Him to manifest His glory in our physical world.

Miracle prayers are bold. They challenge the natural order and call for divine interruption. When we pray for miracles, we are not asking God to do something difficult, we are asking Him to do something divine. A miracle is a supernatural intervention of God in the affairs of men. Whether it's healing, a supernatural provision, divine protection, or deliverance, miracles affirm God's love and power.

When you pray for miracles, let your heart be full of faith. Jesus never performed miracles to entertain or impress but to show compassion and reveal the Kingdom of God. Your prayer must reflect that same motive; a desire for God's will, God's glory, and the good of others.

Effective miracle prayers combine the Word of God and the power of the Holy Spirit. Speak God's promises aloud. Declare the healing Scriptures. Release your faith in Jesus' name. Anoint with oil if led. Lay hands if appropriate. Use the authority of the believer as shown in Mark 16:17-18.

A believer's prayer life must not only be full of requests but full of declarations. Miracle prayer involves commanding the situation in Jesus' name. Jesus said, *"They will lay hands on the sick, and they will recover."* This means healing is not only a possibility; it is a divine promise.

Many are waiting for miracles but never pray for them. Miracles don't just happen, they are born in prayer. Elijah prayed, and fire came down from heaven. Moses stretched his rod and the sea parted. Peter prayed, and Dorcas came back to life. Prayer preceded every biblical miracle.

God still heals the sick, delivers the oppressed, and raises the dead. But He is looking for people who will pray and believe. Don't just hope for a miracle, pray for one Your faith may be small, but Jesus said even faith like a mustard seed can move mountains (Matthew 17:20).

Sample Prayer for Miracles

Heavenly Father, I thank You because You are the miracle-working God. I come to You in the name of Jesus, declaring that nothing is impossible for You. Lord, I ask for a miracle in my life today. Let Your power break every limitation and override every natural law. In the name of Jesus, I command healing, deliverance, provision, and restoration. According to Mark 16:17-18, I lay hands on the sick and declare healing. I rebuke every disease, every demonic oppression, and every hindrance to my miracle. Lord, show forth Your glory. Let signs and wonders follow. I believe, and I receive. In Jesus' name. Amen.

66

PRAYER FOR DIVINE FAVOR
(PSALM 5:12)

"For You, O Lord, will bless the righteous;
With favor You will surround him as with a shield.

Understanding Divine Favor

Divine favor is the supernatural influence of God upon a person's life that causes doors to open, people to be kind, and situations to work for good even when they are not expected to. It is a spiritual shield that God places upon His children to distinguish them, protect them, and elevate them.

Favor is not something we earn; it is granted by God in His mercy and love. When we walk in righteousness, as Psalm 5:12 declares, we align ourselves with the conditions that attract divine favor.

The favor of God brings acceleration where there is delay, promotion without compromise, and blessings even in famine.

It surrounds the righteous like a shield, meaning it is constant, protective, and visible.

Examples of Divine Favor in the Bible

- *Esther* found favor in the sight of the king and was elevated to become queen (Esther 2:17).
- *Joseph* had favor with Potiphar, with the prison warden, and eventually with Pharaoh, despite difficult circumstances (Genesis 39:21, 41:40).
- *Mary*, the mother of Jesus, was greeted as one *"highly favored"* (Luke 1:28), chosen to carry The Savior of the world.

These examples show us that favor can bring divine positioning, restoration, honor, and supernatural help.

Why We Need to Pray for Divine Favor

The world is filled with opposition, competition, and unforeseen barriers. But favor can make things happen faster, smoother, and with less struggle. It causes people to help you without knowing why. When God's favor is upon you:

- You are accepted where others are rejected.
- You are preferred where others are ignored.
- You are celebrated where others are tolerated

Favor opens the door that effort and merit alone cannot.

How to Position Yourself for Divine Favor

Walk in righteousness; Psalm 5:12 says God blesses the righteous.

Stay humble and obedient; Favor flows in the path of humility (Proverbs 3:34).

Be prayerful and expectant; Divine favor answers to prayer and faith.

Speak God's promises daily; Declare His favor over your life using Scripture.

Prayer Points for Divine Favor

1. Lord, thank You for surrounding me with Your favor like a shield.
2. Father, let Your favor speak for me where I cannot speak for myself.
3. Let divine favor distinguish me and promote me beyond my qualifications.
4. Lord, open doors of opportunity by Your favor, even in unlikely places.
5. Father, cause those in authority to look upon me with favor, in Jesus' Name.
6. Let the favor that lifted Joseph in Egypt rest upon me and my household.
7. Surround my children and family with Your favor wherever they go.
8. Cancel every word or plan of rejection against me; let Your favor speak louder.

9. Anoint me with favor in business, ministry, and relationships.
10. Let every garment of disfavor be replaced with garments of Your glory.

A Personal Prayer

Heavenly Father, I come before You in the Name of Jesus, acknowledging that You are the source of favor and blessings. Your Word in Psalm 5:12 declares that You surround the righteous with favor like a shield. I thank You for this promise, and I receive it by faith.

Let Your favor go before me today and every day. Open doors that no man can shut. Cause me to be preferred, accepted, remembered, and helped. Shield me from the arrows of rejection, hatred, and disapproval.

Let divine favor rest upon my name, my hands, and my steps. Wherever I go, let Your favor announce me. Raise voices to speak in my favor, and let helpers rise from the north, south, east, and west.

In times of drought, let Your favor be my rain. In moments of challenge, let Your favor lift me. I declare that I am surrounded, shielded, and saturated with divine favor in Jesus' Name. Amen.

67

PRAYER FOR SUPERNATURAL PROVISION
(PHILIPPIANS 4:19)

"And my God shall supply all your need
according to His riches in glory by Christ Jesus."

Supernatural provision is God supplying your needs in ways that transcend natural expectations. It is not limited to the boundaries of salary, savings, or human help. When we pray for supernatural provision, we are acknowledging God as our ultimate Source: Jehovah Jireh, the Lord Who provides.

The Apostle Paul confidently declared in Philippians 4:19 that *"my God shall supply all your need"*, not from the economy of this world, but *"according to His riches in Glory by Christ Jesus."* These are divine, inexhaustible riches; spiritual, material, physical, and emotional.

This kind of prayer is a prayer based on covenant relationship and Kingdom understanding. It stands upon the promises of God, knowing that He takes pleasure in the prosperity of His servants (Psalm 35:27).

Prayers for supernatural provision often arise when the vision is bigger than your resources. In such moments, we must resist fear and anxiety. Faith is the currency of Heaven. We must pray in faith, declare the Word, and trust God for divine intervention.

Many examples in Scripture show us how God intervenes to provide supernaturally:

- Ravens fed Elijah in the wilderness.
- Manna fed the Israelites in the desert.
- A widow's oil kept flowing until every jar was filled.
- Jesus Christ fed multitudes with a few loaves and fish.

God hasn't changed. What He did before, He can do again for you. This prayer opens the door for such divine interventions.

Prayer Focus Points

- Lord, I acknowledge You as my Source and Provider.
- I reject every form of fear, lack, and anxiety.
- Supply all my needs according to Your riches in glory.
- Let hidden treasures and resources be revealed to me.
- Position me to receive divine opportunities and favor.
- Command men and angels to bring my provision.
- Open doors that no man can shut concerning my finances.

Use these prayer points to build a lifestyle of expectancy. Don't pray only once, be persistent. Supernatural provision often meets those who are consistent in prayer and obedience.

Prophetic Declarations

- *I declare that my God supplies all my needs, according to His riches in Glory by Christ Jesus!*
- *I am not limited by my job, location, or background.*
- *I walk in divine provision and supernatural overflow.*
- *Lack and poverty are under my feet.*
- *I am a channel of blessings to others.*
- *I receive creative ideas and divine instructions for wealth.*
- *I see doors opening now in Jesus' name!*

There is power in aligning your tongue with God's Word. Declare these truths daily. Supernatural provision responds to faith-filled words and actions.

Scripture References for Meditation

- Philippians 4:19 *"And my God shall supply all your need..."*
- 2 Corinthians 9:8 *"And God is able to make all grace abound toward you, that you, always having all sufficiency in all things, may have an abundance for every good work."*
- Psalm 23:1 *"The Lord is my shepherd; I shall not want."*
- Deuteronomy 28:11-12 *"The Lord will grant you abundant prosperity..."*

Soak yourself in these Scriptures. Speak them. Pray them. Believe them. Let your heart be at rest, God will provide.

68

PRAYER FOR OPEN HEAVENS
(MALACHI 3:10)

"Bring all the tithes into the storehouse,
that there may be food in My house,
and try Me now in this," Says the LORD of hosts,
"If I will not open for you the windows of heaven
And pour out for you such blessing
That there will not be room enough to receive it."

The concept of *open heavens* in Scripture refers to divine access, favor, and unrestrained flow of God's blessings and presence. When the heavens are open over a person, family, or community, there is an evident manifestation of God's intervention, supply, guidance, and supernatural breakthroughs.

In Malachi 3:10, God gives a direct invitation to His people to test Him through their obedience in giving. He promises a profound result: open heavens and a blessing so great that it cannot be contained. This kind of blessing is not limited to money, it covers all areas of life: spiritual, emotional, physical, and material.

Many believers experience dryness or delay because the heavens seem *closed*. When we talk about *open heavens*, we are talking about a spiritual realm where God's Glory and supply flow unhindered. It is where prayers are answered quickly, direction is clear, resources flow in due season, and heaven's influence is felt on earth.

What Causes the Heavens to Open?

Obedience to God's Word: As stated in Malachi 3:10, tithing and giving with a sincere heart invites open heavens.

Persistent Prayer: Jesus Christ prayed, and the heavens opened (Luke 3:21). Prayer is a key to unlocking heaven's flow.

Sacrificial Living: When Cornelius prayed and gave alms continually, God remembered him (Acts 10:1-4).

Holiness and Hunger for God: A lifestyle of purity and deep hunger for God provokes divine encounters.

Thanksgiving and Praise: Worship shifts the atmosphere and opens heavenly gates (Psalm 100:4).

Benefits of Open Heavens

Abundant Provision: God supplies not just enough, but more than enough (Malachi 3:10).

Revelation and Guidance: You begin to see visions, hear God's voice, and receive divine strategies.

Favor and Opportunities: Doors open without your effort. Grace speak for you.

Spiritual Refreshing: There's a tangible presence of God that renews strength and joy.

Protection from Devourers: The enemy's plans are rebuked by God Himself (Malachi 3:11).

Living under open heavens is living in the supernatural rhythm of grace, favor, and divine alignment.

Prayer Points for Open Heavens

1. *Father, I thank You for Your Word and promises of open heavens in my life.*
2. *Lord, forgive me and have mercy on me for every act of disobedience that may have closed the heavens over me.*
3. *In the name of Jesus, I align my heart and my resources with Your will; let the windows of heaven open over me.*
4. *Every devourer assigned to consume my harvest, be rebuked now by the voice of God!*
5. *I command every spiritual blockage over my destiny to break open, in Jesus' name.*
6. *Let there be rain of abundance, favor, and divine ideas upon my life and family.*
7. *Father, as I honor You with my tithes and offerings, open the heavens and pour out blessings I cannot contain.*
8. *Let Your light break forth over every dark area of my life; shine and release Your glory.*
9. *Holy Spirit, teach me to give, pray, and walk in obedience so I can live under open heavens daily.*

10. *Lord, open the heavens over my church, my city, and my nation. Let revival break out! in Jesus' name, Amen.*

Declarations for Open Heavens

I live under an open heaven, where nothing good is withheld from me.

The Lord is my Source. I will not lack any good thing.

My tithes and offerings speak for me in the courts of heaven.

I walk in divine favor, divine health, and divine opportunities.

Every devourer is rebuked for my sake. My finances, health, and purpose are preserved.

My prayers are not hindered. They ascend swiftly, and answers descend like rain.

I am blessed to be a blessing. I walk in abundance and overflow.

The heavens are open over my family, my work, and my ministry.

I receive the rain of wisdom, insight, and revelation from heaven.

I declare: The windows of heaven are open, and I receive more than I can contain! in Jesus' name, Amen.

69

PRAYER FOR ANGELIC ASSISTANCE
(PSALM 91:11)

"For He shall give His angels charge over you,
to keep you in all your ways."

God's Invisible Army on Assignment

From the beginning of time, angels have been God's messengers and servants, executing His divine purposes on earth. Scripture gives us many examples of angelic interventions: they shut the lions' mouths for Daniel, led Peter out of prison, and stood by Paul in the storm. Psalm 91:11 reminds us that angelic assistance is not just a story of the past but a present reality for those who dwell in the secret place of the Most High.

We are not alone in our journey. God has assigned angels to protect us, guide us, and minister to us. As we walk in obedience and prayer, we can activate divine protection by invoking God's promise to send His angels on assignment.

Angelic Assistance Is Scriptural

Angelic help is not wishful thinking; it is rooted in God's Word. Consider these verses:

Hebrews 1:14 *"Are they not all ministering spirits sent forth to minister for those who will inherit salvation?"*

Acts 12:7 *"Now behold, an angel of the Lord stood by him, and a light shone in the prison..."*

Matthew 4:11 *"Then the devil left Him, and behold, angels came and ministered to Him."*

These examples show us that angels are active in the affairs of the righteous. We do not worship angels, but we recognize their divine purpose in God's Kingdom.

Conditions for Angelic Intervention

Dwelling in God's Presence

Psalm 91 begins with a condition: *"He who dwells in the secret place of the Most High..."* (v.1). Angelic assistance is not automatic for everyone. It is reserved for those who live in close communion with God.

Walking in His Ways

The promise in Psalm 91:11 says angels will *"keep you in all your ways."* These "ways" must be God's ways not the path of sin, rebellion, or compromise.

Living by Faith

Faith activates angelic assignments. When we declare the Word and trust in God's protection, angels are released to enforce His promises.

How to Pray for Angelic Assistance

Here is a sample prayer for activating divine protection and angelic support:

Heavenly Father, I thank You for Your Word that declares You will give Your angels charge over me, to keep me in all my ways. I claim this promise today in the name of Jesus. I dwell in Your secret place, and I trust in Your covering. Let Your angels surround me and my family; protect us in every journey, defend us from every snare, and guide our steps in righteousness. Send angels to fight for me in spiritual battles, to open doors where they are shut, and to minister strength in moments of weakness. I reject every fear, because I am not alone. Thank You, Lord, for angelic assistance. In Jesus' mighty name, Amen.

You can personalize this prayer by inserting names, specific situations, or needs for divine intervention.

Encounters and Testimonies

Many believers today can testify of supernatural escapes, divine warnings, or help that came at just the right time; some without realizing that angels were involved. One may wake up from a dream with a strong sense of divine direction, or a child may be mysteriously saved from danger. These moments are often signs of angelic activity.

While we are not to seek angels, we are to seek God, who commands His angels. As we stay aligned with Him, He deploys them for our good.

Declare These Scriptures Daily

"The angel of the Lord encamps all around those who fear Him, and delivers them." Psalm 34:7

"Bless the Lord, you His angels, who excel in strength, who do His word, heeding the voice of His word." Psalm 103:20

"No evil shall befall you, nor shall any plague come near your dwelling; for He shall give His angels charge over you…" Psalm 91:10-11

Let these verses be a part of your prayer and declaration routine. As you declare God's Word, angels respond.

Living in Awareness of the Invisible

It is time for the Church to walk in the awareness of the spiritual realm. We are not helpless, nor are we alone. With angelic support, we can walk boldly into our assignments, knowing heaven is backing us.

May you walk with confidence that God's angels are with you, guarding, guiding, and fighting for you.

70

PRAYER FOR THE SECOND COMING OF CHRIST
(REVELATION 22:20)

"He who testifies to these things says,
'Surely I am coming quickly.'
Amen. Even so, come, Lord Jesus!"

One of the final prayers recorded in the Bible is a passionate cry: *"Even so, come, Lord Jesus!"* It reflects the deep yearning of the Church for the return of the Bridegroom. This kind of prayer is both a declaration of hope and a call for readiness.

The Second Coming of Christ is not just a theological event; it is the blessed hope of every believer. To pray for His return is to align our hearts with eternity and live with urgency, faith, and holiness.

Living in Expectation

The early Church lived in anticipation of the Lord's return. They preached it, they longed for it, and they prayed for it. Their understanding of the times was shaped by the promise of His coming. For them, this was not just doctrine; it was motivation for purity, endurance, and evangelism.

Today, many believers live as though they don't know Christ is coming back. But those who understand the prophetic calendar of God know that the return of Jesus is imminent. He will come again; not as a servant but as the conquering King. Therefore, we pray:

"Maranatha! Come, Lord Jesus!"

Why Pray for His Coming?

It keeps our hearts anchored in eternity

When we pray for His return, we declare that our citizenship is in heaven (Philippians 3:20).

It fuels holiness.

"And everyone who has this hope in Him purifies himself, just as He is pure." (1 John 3:3)

It stirs evangelism.

Knowing that time is short, we become more passionate in preaching the gospel to the lost.

It partners with God's prophetic agenda.

Just as intercession preceded His first coming, so will it usher in His second coming.

The Spirit and the Bride Say, "Come!"

Revelation 22:17 says, *"And the Spirit and the bride say, 'Come!'"* This is not just a cry for the Lord to return; it is a twofold call:

1. A cry to the world to come and receive eternal life.
2. A cry to Christ to fulfill His promise and return.

This dual call means that while we long for the return of Jesus, we also labor to bring others into the Kingdom. Prayer for His coming includes both evangelistic zeal and prophetic longing.

How to Pray This Kind of Prayer

With Worship and Surrender

Begin with adoration, acknowledging Christ as the Alpha and the Omega. Surrender your heart to Him afresh, laying aside every distraction.

With Repentance and Readiness

Ask the Lord to search your heart. Pray for purity, integrity, and alertness. Like the five wise virgins, we must keep our lamps burning (Matthew 25:1-13).

With Intercession for the Nations

Pray that the Gospel will be preached in every nation as a witness (Matthew 24:14), and that the hearts of men will be turned to God in these last days.

With Faith in His Promise

Declare His Word: *"Surely I am coming quickly."* (Revelation 22:20) Agree with heaven: *"Even so, come, Lord Jesus!"*

Sample Prayer

Father in Heaven, I thank You for the promise of Jesus' return. Your Word is true, and Your timing is perfect.

Lord Jesus, I echo the cry of the Spirit and the Bride: Come! Let the heavens be opened. Let every eye see You in glory. Let every knee bow and every tongue confess that You are Lord.

Prepare my heart. Make me ready. Help me to be found faithful when You return.

Pour out the Spirit of revival and repentance across the nations. Let Your gospel go forth with power to every tribe and tongue.

Strengthen the Church. Purify Your bride. Remove compromise, lukewarmness, and fear.

Come, Lord Jesus. Establish Your Kingdom. Reign in righteousness.

I long for Your appearing. I watch for You. I wait with joy.

In Jesus' name, Amen.

PART 3

GROWING
IN PRAYER

DEVELOPING A CONSISTENT PRAYER LIFE

"Pray without ceasing."
1 Thessalonians 5:17

A consistent prayer life is not a gift for a few, but a discipline available to all. Every believer is invited to live in daily fellowship with God. Prayer is not merely an emergency lifeline or a church ritual; it is the breath of the spiritual man.

To grow in prayer, we must learn to be intentional. Jesus Christ rose early to pray (Mark 1:35), and Daniel had specific times of prayer daily (Daniel 6:10). These are examples of consistency in prayer.

"Now in the morning, having risen a long while before daylight, He went out and departed to a solitary place; and there He prayed." Mark 1:35

If our Lord Jesus needed time alone with the Father, how much more do we?

The enemy's tactic is to crowd your life with noise and busyness, so that prayer becomes optional. But those who grow in grace know that everything must start and end in prayer. It becomes a way of life.

"Evening and morning and at noon I will pray, and cry aloud, and He shall hear my voice." Psalm 55:17

We see that David had a rhythm. Morning, noon, and night; he communed with the Lord. You may not start with three times a day, but begin with what is realistic for you. The key is consistency.

Whether it is 10 minutes in the morning or praying during your commute, keep it steady. Prayer is a relationship.

"But you, when you pray, go into your room, and when you have shut your door, pray to your Father who is in the secret place; and your Father who sees in secret will reward you openly." Matthew 6:6

The secret place is the consistent place. Many want public power without private prayer. But the Lord rewards the one who seeks Him in quiet. This is where consistency is built; in the daily shutting of the door, the daily returning to the feet of Jesus.

Create a place and time. Let that spot become your altar. Build your prayer altar brick by brick, word by word, day by day.

"Then He spoke a parable to them, that men always ought to pray and not lose heart." Luke 18:1

Consistency in prayer is not based on emotion, but on devotion. The Lord Jesus taught us to pray always; this means prayer must become part of our normal routine.

Don't wait for a crisis to start. Prayer is a shield before the storm, not just a rescue during it. A consistent prayer life prepares your heart to hear God, resist temptation, and walk in victory.

LEARNING TO PRAY IN THE SPIRIT

Prayer is a divine language. As believers, we are not only called to pray, but to grow deeper in prayer, more intimate, and Spirit-led. One powerful dimension of growth in prayer is learning to pray in the Spirit.

"Praying always with all prayer and supplication in the Spirit, being watchful to this end with all perseverance and supplication for all the saints." Ephesians 6:18

This command is part of the believer's armor. Paul encourages us to pray in the Spirit at all times. But what does that mean?

To pray in the Spirit is to pray under the influence, guidance, and inspiration of the Holy Spirit. It is not limited to praying in tongues, though praying in tongues is one way of doing it. It also includes praying with understanding while being led by the Spirit in content, tone, and burden.

"For if I pray in a tongue, my spirit prays, but my understanding is unfruitful. What is the conclusion then? I will pray with the spirit, and I will also pray with the understanding." 1 Corinthians 14:14-15a

Paul mentions two important modes of prayer: with the spirit and with the understanding. Praying in the Spirit includes praying in tongues, where your human mind may not grasp the words, but your spirit is in full communion with God.

However, praying in the Spirit is more than spiritual language. It is spiritual alignment; your mind, will, and emotions surrender to the Holy Spirit. You become an instrument through which the Spirit intercedes and groans for the will of God to be done on earth.

"Likewise the Spirit also helps in our weaknesses. For we do not know what we should pray for as we ought, but the Spirit Himself makes intercession for us with groanings which cannot be uttered." Romans 8:26

When we pray in the Spirit, we overcome the limitations of human knowledge. Sometimes, we don't know what is ahead, what to pray, or how to express our burdens. The Holy Spirit steps in to intercede through us.

Praying in the Spirit also *builds us up spiritually:*

"But you, beloved, building yourselves up on your most holy faith, praying in the Holy Spirit." Jude 1:20

Every time we pray in the Spirit, we edify ourselves. Our faith is strengthened. Our inner being is revived. It's like charging a spiritual battery.

We receive *revelation*, clarity, and divine direction. The Spirit helps us stay in line with God's will and resist distractions.

How can one learn to pray in the Spirit?

Desire it: Ask the Holy Spirit to help you pray more deeply.

Stay in the Word: The Word and the Spirit work together.

Pray in tongues regularly: If you have the gift, use it often.

Practice stillness: Learn to wait and listen during prayer.

Yield your will: Let the Spirit lead you away from routine into intimacy.

The more you do it, the easier it becomes. Like a river flowing from within, you will begin to sense the Spirit's leading in what to pray, how to pray, and even how long to pray.

Sometimes, He may lead you into strong intercession, other times into deep worship or silent weeping. All of it is prayer in the Spirit.

As you grow in this area, prayer becomes less of a duty and more of a *delight*. You begin to enjoy unbroken fellowship with God.

"God is Spirit, and those who worship Him must worship in Spirit and truth." John 4:24

Praying in the Spirit is not a theological concept; it is a *spiritual reality* every believer can and must walk in.

You can move from dry and routine prayers into refreshing and effective communication with the Father, led by His Spirit.

Ask the Lord daily: *"Holy Spirit, help me to pray."* And as you yield, you will grow in power, purpose, and partnership with Him in prayer.

THE POWER OF FASTING AND PRAYER

Fasting and prayer is one of the most powerful spiritual combinations in the life of a believer. While prayer connects us with God and His will, fasting humbles the flesh and brings your spirit into greater sensitivity. It is not a religious routine, but a divine strategy for breakthrough, revelation, and power.

In Matthew 6:17-18 Jesus Christ says,

"But you, when you fast, anoint your head and wash your face, so that you do not appear to men to be fasting, but to your Father Who is in the secret place; and your Father Who sees in secret will reward you openly."

Fasting is assumed here, not suggested. Jesus did not say *"if"* but *"when"*. This shows us that fasting is expected in our walk with God. Fasting is not to be done for men to see but unto God. It invites a divine response and open rewards.

Fasting is about aligning ourselves to hear and obey God better. In Acts 13:2-3, the early Church gives us a clear example:

"As they ministered to the Lord and fasted, the Holy Spirit said, 'Now separate to Me Barnabas and Saul for the work to which I have called them.' Then, having fasted and prayed, and laid hands on them, they sent them away."

Here, fasting opened the way for direction and the release of divine assignments. It was while they were fasting and ministering that the voice of the Spirit became clear. Fasting clears the spiritual atmosphere, making it easier to discern God's instructions.

In some situations, spiritual resistance cannot be broken without fasting. Jesus taught His disciples this in Matthew 17:21

"However, this kind does not go out except by prayer and fasting."

There are *"kinds"* of spiritual opposition that only respond to this deeper level of consecration. Fasting intensifies the anointing and enhances the authority with which we deal with spiritual matters.

Even in the Old Testament, we see the power of fasting. In Ezra 8:23 *"So we fasted and entreated our God for this, and He answered our prayer."*

God answers when we seek Him with fasting and humility. Fasting also brings repentance, healing, and restoration to communities and nations.

In Joel 2:12, God calls His people: *"Now, therefore,"* says the Lord, *"Turn to Me with all your heart, with fasting, with weeping, and with mourning."*

Fasting is a language of urgency. It is a cry from the heart that says, *"Lord, we need You now."* When done sincerely, it brings God's favor and visitation.

Jesus Christ Himself fasted for 40 days in (Luke 4:1-2). If the Son of God needed to fast before entering His assignment, how much more do we? Fasting prepared Him to overcome temptations and operate in the power of the Spirit.

Luke 4:14 *"Then Jesus returned in the power of the Spirit to Galilee, and news of Him went out through all the surrounding region."*

Fasting does not earn us power, but it positions us to receive it. It quiets the noise of the flesh and sharpens the voice of the Spirit. It deepens our hunger for God and aligns us with His purposes.

Isaiah 58 reveals God's heart on true fasting. Verses 6-8 say:

"Is this not the fast that I have chosen:
To loose the bonds of wickedness,
To undo the heavy burdens,
To let the oppressed go free,
And that you break every yoke?
Is it not to share your bread with the hungry,
And that you bring to your house the poor who are cast out...
Then your light shall break forth like the morning..."

True fasting brings transformation; not only personal but social. It is a tool for revival, spiritual growth, and divine empowerment.

HOW TO BUILD A STRONG PRAYER ALTAR

A prayer altar is more than a physical location; it is a sacred spiritual discipline. It is a place of consistent communion and covenant with God, where Heaven touches earth and destinies are shaped. Every believer must learn how to raise and maintain a powerful prayer altar to remain strong in the Spirit, overcome life's battles, and walk in divine purpose.

Throughout Scripture, we see the importance of altars. Patriarchs like Abraham, Isaac, Jacob, and Elijah all raised altars, places of divine encounter and sacrifice. Your prayer altar must become your secret place of power, where you meet with the Living God daily.

"But you, when you pray, go into your room, and when you have shut your door, pray to your Father Who is in the secret place; and your Father Who sees in secret will reward you openly." Matthew 6:6

1. Understand What a Prayer Altar Is

A prayer altar is a dedicated lifestyle of consistent communication with God. It's not just a morning devotion or an emergency hotline when trouble hits, it's a fire that burns continually in your heart and home.

"The fire shall ever be burning upon the altar; it shall never go out." Leviticus 6:13

Your prayer altar is where:

- You worship and minister to God (Acts 13:2).
- You receive revelation and instruction (Jeremiah 33:3).
- You fight spiritual battles and intercede for others (Ezekiel 22:30).
- You experience personal revival and transformation (Romans 12:1-2).

When your altar is weak, your spiritual life weakens. But when your altar is burning, your life will overflow with divine power, clarity, and victory.

2. Build the Altar With the Word of God

The Word of God is the foundation of every strong prayer altar. Prayer without the Word becomes emotion or repetition. But when you fill your altar with Scripture, you align with heaven and pray the will of God.

"Let the Word of Christ dwell in you richly in all wisdom..."
Colossians 3:16

Declare and meditate on the Word daily. Use it to shape your prayers:

- *Pray God's promises* (2 Corinthians 1:20).
- *Use Psalms* to worship and pour out your heart (Psalm 42).
- *Intercede with apostolic prayers* like in Ephesians 1:17-19 and Colossians 1:9-12.
- *Speak the Word* into your circumstances (Ezekiel 37:4).

Let your prayer altar be a Word-saturated place where the voice of God speaks clearly.

3. Be Consistent: Schedule It

Building a strong altar requires discipline. You cannot grow spiritually with a random or emotional prayer life. Like Daniel, who prayed three times a day, set a time and stick to it; morning, midday, or/and night.

"Now when Daniel knew that the writing was signed, he went home. And in his upper room... he knelt down on his knees three times that day, and prayed and gave thanks before his God, as was his custom since early days." Daniel 6:10

Our Lord Jesus Christ *"Now in the morning, having risen a long while before daylight, He went out and departed to a solitary place; and there He prayed."* Mark 1:35

Choose your time. Make it sacred. Let heaven know to meet you there daily. When prayer becomes part of your rhythm, your altar becomes a throne room experience.

4. Include Praise, Worship, and Thanksgiving

Every altar must have the fragrance of Worship. It draws God's presence and prepares the ground for prayer. Thanksgiving strengthens your faith and turns your focus from problems to the greatness of God.

"Enter into His gates with thanksgiving, and into His courts with praise. Be thankful to Him, and bless His name." Psalm 100:4

Start your prayer with worship. Let songs, Psalms, and words of adoration rise. This is not a routine, it is how we exalt God and host His presence.

"But You are holy, enthroned in the praises of Israel." Psalm 22:3

A strong altar is a throne of praise, and God inhabits that throne.

5. Add Fasting and Sacrifice to Your Altar

To deepen your altar, God may call you into fasting and sacrificial living; offering up what costs you something. These sacrifices are not to earn God's favor, but to position yourself for deeper spiritual sensitivity and surrender.

"Is this not the fast that I have chosen: To loose the bonds of wickedness... and that you break every yoke?" Isaiah 58:6

When Elijah repaired the altar and added the sacrifice, fire fell from heaven.

"Then Elijah said to all the people, 'Come near to me.' So all the people came near to him. And he repaired the altar of the Lord that was broken down... Then the fire of the Lord fell..." 1 Kings 18:30,38

The altar without sacrifice is incomplete. Sacrifice releases fire!

What Are the Sacrifices on the Altar?

Your Body (Physical Obedience);

Offer your time, energy, and discipline in prayer. Push past tiredness and comfort to seek God.

"I beseech you therefore, brethren... present your bodies a living sacrifice, holy, acceptable to God..." Romans 12:1

Your Time.

Sacrificing sleep to pray early or staying up late to seek God. Give Him the first and best portion of your day.

"O God, You are my God; Early will I seek You..." Psalm 63:1

Food (Fasting).

Regular fasting to humble the flesh and sharpen your spirit. It creates space for revelation and breakthrough.

"However, this kind does not go out except by prayer and fasting." Matthew 17:21

Your Comfort and Agenda.

Sacrificing your own plans to yield to His will. Letting go of what you want in exchange for what God wants.

"Not My will, but Yours, be done." Luke 22:42

Your Possessions (Generosity and Giving).

Giving to the poor, supporting God's work, or blessing others in need. Every giving at the altar becomes a sweet aroma to God.

"And do not forget to do good and to share, for with such sacrifices God is well pleased." Hebrews 13:16

Your Praise and Thanksgiving.

Praise becomes a precious offering to God.

"Therefore by Him let us continually offer the sacrifice of praise to God..." Hebrews 13:15

Your Will (Obedience to God's Word);

When you obey God's voice, you offer your will as a sacrifice, and He honors it.

"To obey is better than sacrifice, and to heed than the fat of rams." 1 Samuel 15:22

6. Keep the Fire Burning

An altar is not built once; it is maintained daily. Your fire must be protected from busyness, distractions, and sin. You keep it burning by praying in the Spirit, staying in the Word, and walking in holiness.

"Pray without ceasing." 1 Thessalonians 5:17

"But you, beloved, building yourselves up on your most holy faith, praying in the Holy Spirit..." Jude 1:20

Guard your altar. Renew it when it feels dry. Help others around you also build altars; your family, children, leaders, and Church.

A strong prayer altar will bring personal revival, family restoration, divine direction, protection, and power for ministry.

MAKING PRAYER A LIFESTYLE

A believer's greatest strength is not in how much they know, but in how deeply they pray. Prayer is not just something we do when we have time; it is the very air our spirit breathes. To grow in prayer is to grow in God, and to make prayer a lifestyle is to make God your dwelling place.

1. Constant Fellowship with God

God did not create us for religious routines; He created us for relationship. Prayer is the heart of that relationship. The Bible says:

"Pray without ceasing." 1 Thessalonians 5:17

This verse is more than a command; it's an invitation. God is calling us to unbroken fellowship with Him, not just during morning devotions, but in every part of our day. While cooking, walking, driving, working, prayer can continue. Whispering praise, lifting quiet petitions, listening to His Spirit; all these are forms of constant prayer.

2. Jesus Christ, Our Perfect Example

Jesus made prayer a lifestyle. The Son of God, though perfect and sinless, still prioritized time with the Father.

"So He often withdrew into the wilderness and prayed." Luke 5:16

If Jesus Christ needed to pray, how much more do we? The life of Jesus shows us that prayer must be woven into the fabric of our daily lives. His miracles flowed from His secret times with God. Prayer carried the weight of his wisdom, the fire of his boldness, and the warmth of his compassion.

When prayer becomes our lifestyle, we are empowered like Jesus to overcome temptation, walk in love, and fulfill our assignment.

3. Discipline Before Delight

Making prayer a lifestyle begins with discipline. Many believers wait until they "feel like praying." But feelings are not the compass of a spiritual life. The early Church prayed at regular hours (Acts 3:1), and Daniel prayed three times daily (Daniel 6:10), even when it put his life at risk.

"But I discipline my body and bring it into subjection..." 1 Corinthians 9:27a

Start small if you must; ten minutes in the morning, five minutes in the afternoon, fifteen minutes before bed but stay consistent. Prayer schedules help you build spiritual muscles. Over time, what began as a duty becomes a joy.

4. Building an Altar in Your Life

Every believer must build a personal altar of prayer. Not a physical altar of stones, but a spiritual one made of time, sacrifice, and consistency.

"Then he built an altar to the Lord and called on the name of the Lord." Genesis 12:8b

Abraham built altars as he journeyed, and at each one, he encountered God. So must we. Whether it's a quiet corner in your home or a walk in the park, find a space that becomes your meeting place with God. Over time, it becomes sacred; a place where Heaven touches earth.

5. A Lifestyle That Influences Others

When prayer becomes your lifestyle, it doesn't just change you; it changes the atmosphere around you. Your words carry weight. Your decisions reflect wisdom. People begin to sense peace around you. Why? Because you've been with God.

"Now when they saw the boldness of Peter and John... they realized that they had been with Jesus." Acts 4:13

You don't need to announce that you are a person of prayer. The evidence will speak. Your home, your ministry, your business, your children, they will all bear the mark of a praying life.

FINAL ENCOURAGEMENT AND CALL TO PRAYER

As we conclude this journey through the 70 kinds of prayers, let us pause and reflect on the incredible gift God has given us through prayer. Prayer is not a religious routine or a mere obligation; it is a divine privilege, and an open invitation into deep fellowship with the Creator of the universe. Each type of prayer you have encountered in this book opens a door to a dimension of God's heart. Whether it is intercession, thanksgiving, prophetic prayer, travailing prayer, or any other kind, all forms point to one thing: *a relationship with God and His purpose on earth.*

You have not only been informed, but equipped; to stand in the gap, to fight spiritual battles, to minister healing, to worship, to seek direction, to birth revival, and to commune with your Father in Heaven.

Now is the time to rise and pray. Let the knowledge you have received stir your spirit into action. Let your prayer life be marked by diversity, fervency, and consistency. Do not be afraid to step into unfamiliar territories in prayer. The Holy Spirit is your Helper and Teacher. He will guide you into all truth and train your hands for spiritual warfare.

Start small but be intentional. Establish a personal altar. Create a schedule. Set prayer goals. Let prayer become your first response, not your last resort. As you pray, expect answers. Expect transformation. Expect heaven to move on your behalf.

The Church is strengthened through prayer. Families are healed through prayer. Nations are saved through prayer. Personal destinies are unlocked through prayer. Miracles are released through prayer. The sick are restored, the lost are found through prayer.

God is looking for intercessors. Will you be one? He is searching for worshipers. Will you respond? He is seeking those who will travail for souls, watch over cities, and pray without ceasing. There is a cry in the Spirit: *"Who will stand in the gap?"* Let your answer be, "Here I am, Lord. Teach me to pray."

No one is born a prayer warrior. We all grow into it. And we grow by doing, by praying. You may not feel strong or skilled, but God delights in your heart's desire to seek Him.

Do not let your environment, your past, your personality, or your schedule silence your prayer life. Prayer changes you first before it changes your circumstances. Let every day be saturated with the atmosphere of prayer; morning, noon, and night. Whether alone or with others, in the car or at the altar, God is listening.

I encourage you to revisit these 70 kinds of prayer often. Make them part of your spiritual discipline. Use them in your devotion, your ministry, your warfare, your worship, and your daily walk with the Lord. There is no limit to what God can do through a praying believer.

Now, go forward in boldness. Be a firebrand of intercession. Be a vessel of revival. Be a voice crying in the wilderness. Let the anointing of prayer rest upon you, and may the Spirit of grace and supplication pour upon you mightily.

Pray without ceasing.
Pray with purpose.
Pray with power.

Amen.

INVITATION

Our righteousness is of the Lord. It is therefore necessary for us to be part of the body of Christ and to have a personal relationship with the Lord to become children of God.

John 1:12-13 *"But as many as received Him, to them gave He power to become the sons of God, even to them that believe on His name: Which were born, not of blood, nor of the will of the flesh, nor of the will of man, but of God."*

Do you want to be confident in your spiritual battles in prayer, do you want to give your heart and your life to God so He can dwell in you for ever? You can pray the following prayer to the Lord.

Heavenly Father, I come to You through Your only begotten Son Jesus Christ. I am very sorry for my sins, I repent of my sins and iniquities. Please forgive me, cleanse me from all my unrighteousness through the Blood of Your Son Jesus Christ. I want You to come into my heart and save me. Lord Jesus, I believe you died on the cross for my sins and was raised again for my justification. I receive You as the Lord and Master of my life. I ask You to lead and guide me every day in Your Word and I ask for the power to obey you. I choose to obey you and follow Your will for my life. Thank You Lord for coming into my heart. Thank You Holy Spirit for writing my name in the Lamb's book of Life. In Jesus' Name I pray. Amen.

If you are a Christian already and you want to enter into the victorious life of Christ, to be set free from the powers of darkness and from the dominion of sin. You want to renew your commitment and covenant with the Lord you can likewise pray the above prayer.

If you need to agree in prayer with a minister to help you more in your prayer life and in your spiritual battles, write or call us, and we shall be delighted to assist you more in the Name of Our Lord Jesus Christ.

All our contact details can be found in the website www.shekinahevangelicalchurch.com

ABOUT THE AUTHOR

The author of this book: Pastor Mariana Vanstipelen is a seasoned Bible teacher and passionate intercessor, dedicated to equipping believers with the power of prayer. With a deep love for the Word of God, she has taught and led prayer ministries, inspiring many to seek God wholeheartedly.

Pastor Mariana was born again while completing her Master's Degree in 1991. She fully devoted herself to being a disciple of the Lord Jesus Christ and prioritized studying God's Word above all subjects. Fluent in eight languages, Mariana is dedicated to using her linguistic abilities to share God's Word with the nations.

To God be the Glory.

OTHER BOOKS BY THE SAME AUTHOR

1. Biblical Principles of Long Life
2. Converting Mistakes to Miracles
3. Seven Ways God Answers Prayers
4. The Creative Power of Prayer
5. Prayer for Healing
6. The Impact of Fasting in Prayer
7. Faith Versus Fear
8. Forgive
9. A Happy Christian
10. Jesus-Christ, the Bread of Life
11. Jesus-Christ, the Word of God
12. Power to Prosper
13. The Fruit of the Spirit
14. The Hem of His Garment
15. The Holy Spirit
16. The King of kings
17. Teenagers
18. The Mantle of Power
19. The Rhema of God
20. The Shekinah of God

BLESSINGS

As you close the pages of 70 *Kinds of Prayers*,
may a fresh fire be ignited in your spirit.
May your prayer life never be the same again.
I pray that as you grow in understanding and practice
of these diverse ways to commune with God,
Heaven will open over you in new dimensions.

May your prayers rise like incense before the Lord;
powerful, effective, and full of faith. Whether you are praying
in intercession, thanksgiving, travail, warfare, or any other
of the 70 kinds, may you experience the nearness of God
and the joy of answered prayer.

If this book has blessed you, we encourage you to share
your testimony. Let others be strengthened by your story,
and let your journey inspire a generation of praying believers.

And remember, you are not alone in this sacred calling to pray.
We welcome your prayer requests and stand with you,
believing God to move mountains, heal hearts,
and fulfill every divine promise. As James 5:16 says,
"The effective, fervent prayer of a righteous man avails much."

May the Lord bless you and keep you;
May He make His face shine upon you and be gracious to you;
May He lift up His countenance upon you and give you peace.
You are anointed to pray. You are chosen to intercede.
You are empowered to see Heaven touch earth.

NOTES